Praise for This Book

"The best primer we've ~~en."—*Forbes Magazine, Spring 2000 Special Issue*

"Should be required reading for anybody receiving options as compensation."—*Roy Lewis, co-author, The Motley Fool's Investment Tax Guide 2000*

From our message board. *#3931:* "I think it has saved me a lot on taxes already, so thank you!" *#4226:* "It has thorough coverage of all the issues, yet is very easy to read!" *#4610: "Consider Your Options* is the best book on the subject." *#4817:* "The book is terrific and very useful. I've recommended it to many colleagues." *#4831:* "Thanks for your thoroughly enlightening book *Consider Your Options.* I learned a lot about equity compensation from it." *#4950:* "Buying your book is probably the best investment I have ever made. Thank you."

Praise for Our Web Site

"One of our favorite sites."—*Newsweek Magazine,*

"One of the top 50 financial web sites."—*Money Magazine, December, 1999*

"A good newsy site, easy to navigate and fun to read. Its explanations are crystal clear."—*The Boston Globe, February, 1999*

"You have a right—and an obligation—to understand the tax laws that apply to you."

—*Kaye A. Thomas*

Consider Your Options

Get the Most from Your
Equity Compensation

Kaye A. Thomas

A Plain Language Guide From
FAIRMARK PRESS INC. LISLE, ILLINOIS

Consider Your Options
Get the Most from Your
Equity Compensation

This edition of *Consider Your Options: Get the Most from Your Equity Compensation* reflects relevant legal authorities as of December 31, 1999.

Published by:

Fairmark Press Inc.
P.O. Box 353
Lisle, Illinois 60532

Copyright © 2000 by Kaye A. Thomas
Second Printing 2000
Printed in the United States of America

Cover design by Abacus Graphics, Oceanside, California

Publisher's Cataloging-in-Publication Data
Thomas, Kaye A.
    Consider your options : get the most from your equity compensation / Kaye A. Thomas. -- 1st ed.
      p. cm.
    Includes bibliographical references and index.
    LCCN: 99-91685
    ISBN: 0-9674981-6-3

    1. Employee stock options--Law and legislation--United States--Popular works. 2. Deferred compensation--Taxation--Law and legislation--United States--Popular works. I. Title.

KF6379.Z9T46 2000   343.7305'242
                    QBI99-1864

Table of Contents

About the Author

Kaye Thomas spends his office hours disguised as a mild-mannered tax lawyer. He has nearly 20 years of experience dealing with tax matters relating to business transactions, finance and compensation. Much of that experience is in advising companies on how to establish and maintain equity compensation arrangements, and individuals on how to manage those benefits.

Away from the office, he fights a never-ending battle for truth, justice, and a less taxing American way. He maintains a free web site called the *Tax Guide for Investors* at **www.fairmark.com**, providing hundreds of pages of plain language tax guidance. The web site also features a message board where Kaye and other tax professionals respond to questions and comments from readers.

Kaye's law degree is from Harvard Law School, where he was selected to be an editor of the Harvard Law Review and graduated *cum laude* in 1980.

Acknowledgments

I pause here to thank some of the people who made this book possible.

Barbara Baksa drew on her experience as a Senior Equity Compensation Specialist with E*TRADE Business Solutions to suggest ways to make the book more useful.

The person I called when the tax law had me stumped was Curt Freeman, who always seemed to have the knowledge or insight I needed.

For help on various practical issues in getting the book out, I turned to Joe Hurley, author of *The Best Way to Save for College.*

Jennifer Leib accepted proofreading responsibility but went beyond the call of duty with many suggestions for improvements in the book.

Beth Mowry Thomas is my wife and partner, and also coach, editor, business manager, CPA, therapist . . . more succinctly, this book's *sine qua non.*

None of these people had an opportunity to prevent my evil twin from inserting errors during final editing.

Part I
Laying the Foundation

Part I of this book provides the information you need to get the most out of all the other parts. Chapter 1 explains what's the big deal about *equity compensation*—stock and options—and why it's so important to handle them properly. Chapter 2 provides a bird's-eye view of the entire subject to give you a feel for what's coming.

There are certain things about stock, options and taxes that are almost never explained because "every idiot" knows them. Unfortunately, there are many normal, intelligent, educated adults who *don't* know these things—because hardly anyone ever bothers to explain them. The remaining chapters in Part I lay out the basics in plain language.

Part I Laying the Foundation

Chapter 1
The Buzz—and the Buzz Saw

D'Anne Schjerning worked as a secretary. According to an article in the *Wall Street Journal*, she was able to retire early—as a millionaire. She didn't marry the boss or win the lottery. Nor did she scrimp and save for decades. How did she do it? By exercising stock options she received from her company.

> She's not alone. The same article reports that dozens of companies have millionaire secretaries.

The stock or options you get from your company won't necessarily allow you to move from Baltic Avenue to Boardwalk. They deserve your attention, though. Just about anyone who has access to a stock or option plan can painlessly build up thousands of dollars in value within a few years.

Let's face it: Americans tend to be lousy savers. Most of us spend nearly all of what we earn. Many of us spend *more* than we earn. This is not a good recipe for building wealth. *Equity compensation*—stock and options—provides a way to get over that hump. You can build net worth almost without knowing it. Those option agreements and stock certificates have opportunity written all over them.

Why They Work

The magic word is *growth*. Companies grow. That makes their stock and options go up in value. It's that simple. Whether you work for a startup that's looking to go public or an established industrial giant, growth—specifically, growth in earnings—is the goal. If you hold stock or options, your company's growth will add to your wealth.

Holding stock or options makes you an *investor*, whether or not you're used to thinking of yourself that way. And there's no better investment than owning a piece of the company where you work.

The Unkindest Cut

Investors encounter various types of expenses that reduce their profits. Brokerage commissions, periodicals—even the cost of this book—cut into the amount of wealth you're accumulating. One expense is greater than all the rest: *taxes*.

The good news is that you have a fair amount of control over this expense. You can't change the rules or lower the rates, of course. Yet careful planning can reduce the pain. Generally, *you* determine when to exercise options and when to sell stock. You may have other planning opportunities as well, such as the *Section 83b election*. If you make the right moves, Uncle Sam gets a smaller piece of the pie.

> An extreme example: the *Wall Street Journal* reported in June, 1999 that Margaret Whitman, president of eBay, Inc. (provider of an Internet auction site) may save more than $100 million in taxes through a tax planning technique on her stock options.

Sadly, many holders of stock and options fail to seize these opportunities. They wake up to the fact that they have options when they're about to expire. Exercising the options becomes a fire drill, with no opportunity for planning. Much of the stock has to be sold right away to pay taxes. The beneficiary of this inattention is the United States Treasury.

If you find yourself in this situation, there's still plenty of help in this book, as it explains all the tax rules that apply when you exercise options and sell the stock.

There's still more help here, though, for those who are willing to spend a little time planning their moves. Painful as it may be to study tax rules, the payoff can be handsome indeed.

Good Help Is Hard to Find

As equity compensation gains in popularity, more and more people are affected by these complicated tax rules. Yet the guidance on these rules is skimpy. The IRS puts out scores of information publications explaining all sorts of tax rules in great detail, yet devotes less than two pages in one publication to the tax rules for compensatory options. Alternative minimum tax? The IRS used to have a publication explaining AMT, but discontinued it several years ago.

A qualified tax professional may be able to guide you through the maze. Bear in mind, though, that some return preparers get most of their tax information from IRS publications, and we've already seen how little help they'll get from that source. Even the pros who use more sophisticated research materials may not run into these rules often enough to know all the ins and outs. It's important for *you* to learn these rules, and become part of the team with your tax pro to reduce your tax bill.

www.fairmark.com

Some of the material in this book is drawn from the Fairmark Press *Tax Guide for Investors*, a free web site located at www.fairmark.com. While this book contains material that doesn't appear on the web site, it's also true that some topics touched on briefly here, such as the wash sale rule, receive a more thorough treatment on the web site. You're invited to visit that site for details on related tax issues. Significant developments relating to the topics in this book will be posted there as well. You'll also find a message board at fairmark.com where you can post questions about this subject, or comments (glowing ones, I hope!) about this book.

Chapter 2
The Big Picture

Compensation in stock and options can provide huge advantages for both the company and the workers who receive the compensation. It's fair to say that many companies couldn't survive in today's market without providing this form of compensation. What makes equity compensation better than cash?

Major advantages. Equity compensation helps the company in several ways. Compensation provided in this form doesn't absorb cash that may be needed for other corporate purposes. The company may be able to claim a deduction for the compensation, reducing its taxes and preserving even more cash. In some cases, the company may be able to provide this compensation without taking a "hit" to earnings for accounting purposes. By showing higher earnings the company makes investors happy and increases the market value of its stock.

The most important advantage of equity compensation, though, is its ability to attract, retain and motivate workers who can make the company prosper. Nothing is more important to a company's success than a motivated workforce. Compensation in stock and options gives the workers a real stake in the success of the company, and that's good for both the company and the workers.

Taxes. When it comes to taxes, equity compensation provides both advantages and disadvantages relative to cash. In some situations, it's possible for workers to obtain valuable rights, even amass significant wealth, without having to report income until the rights are cashed in. With cash, it's pay as you go. The flip side is that in some circumstances you *do* have to pay tax on your equity compensation, even before you've reduced your holdings to cash—perhaps even before it's *possible* to reduce your holdings to cash. In this situation you need to come up with money somewhere else to pay taxes on what you received. When this happens, careful planning is a necessity.

Shareholders. It may be useful to have in mind the perspective of other shareholders on compensation in stock and options. When a company issues shares as compensation, it increases the total number of shares outstanding. If the value of the company doesn't increase by a corresponding amount, the value per share is diluted. For this reason, shareholders—especially large, institutional shareholders—may be skeptical about some arrangements for equity compensation. Shareholders are the ultimate bosses of the corporation and generally have the right to approve equity compensation arrangements. If your company is less generous than you would like, it may be at least partly because existing shareholders want to protect their own equity.

Shareholders know, however, that what's good for the company will ultimately be good for them. The advantages mentioned above provide a convincing argument for equity compensation arrangements in general. A well designed program will provide value for *everyone*, including the company's shareholders.

Property as Compensation

You're used to thinking of compensation as cash you receive for your services. Other types of income, such as interest and dividends, typically come in the form of cash, too. It may seem strange at first to report compensation income when you haven't received any cash.

That's exactly what the law requires you to do. The general rule is that whenever you receive stock or other property as compensation for services, you have to report the receipt of compensation income. You may have to report income and come up with money to pay the tax, even though you didn't receive any cash and can't sell the property! In some situations, though, you won't report income until a future event occurs.

If you're an employee, you may have *withholding* on your equity compensation. Of course the company won't withhold shares of stock and send them to the IRS. Somehow or other the withholding obligation has to be satisfied in cash. If you're not an employee (for example, a non-employee director or consultant), the withholding rules don't apply.

The amount of compensation you have to report depends on the *fair market value* of the property you receive. For publicly traded stock, fair market value is determined by the trading price. If your company isn't publicly traded, it may be more difficult to determine fair market value.

Stock Grants and Purchases

Companies sometimes provide equity compensation by making a *stock grant*. They simply give you the stock in return for your services. This is the simplest form of equity compensation, and the result is that you report equity compensation equal to the fair market value of the stock.

This assumes there are no strings attached to the stock grant—in other words, the stock is *vested*. Your company may say that you have to give the stock back if you quit working there within a specified period of time. In that case you don't report income until the end of that time period unless you file a *section 83b election* with the IRS (see Chapter 37). The reason you might do this is to avoid reporting *more* compensation income. If you delay reporting until the stock vests, you have to report compensation income equal to the fair market value of the stock *at that time*, which may be a lot higher than the value when you received it.

These rules apply also when you buy stock from the company. If you buy at a bargain price, you have to report compensation income equal to the difference between fair market value and the amount you paid. Even if you pay full fair market value, you may have to file a section 83b election if you've agreed to sell the stock back to the company under some circumstances.

Nonqualified Options

A *nonqualified option* is an option to buy the company's stock, other than an *incentive stock option* (described below). Companies can grant nonqualified options to employees and other service providers, such as non-employee directors and consultants. The rules for nonqualified options build on the rules for stock grants and purchases.

You don't report any income at the time you receive a nonqualified option. This is true even though the option may be a valuable property right that would result in gift tax if you gave it away. Instead, you generally report income at the time you exercise the option. At that time, you apply all the rules described above for purchases of stock in connection with services. You report compensation income equal to the difference between the fair market value of the stock and the amount you paid. If the stock isn't vested at the time you exercise the option, you won't report income until the stock vests unless you file a section 83b election.

Incentive Stock Options

An *incentive stock option* (ISO) is an option that meets various technical requirements set forth in the Internal Revenue Code. You must be an *employee* to receive an ISO. Non-employee directors and consultants aren't eligible.

The rules for incentive stock options build on the rules for stock grants *and* the rules for nonqualified options. You don't report income when you receive the options *or* when you exercise them and receive the stock. Instead, you report income when you *sell* the stock. Better still, if you hold the stock long enough, you'll be able to report long-term capital gain instead of compensation income. That makes this form of equity compensation very attractive to employees. But there are important qualifications.

One is the special holding period for capital gain treatment. You have to hold the stock until the *later* of two years after you received the option or one year after you exercised it. Otherwise you'll be treated (approximately) the same as if you received and exercised a nonqualified option.

More importantly, although you don't report income when you exercise the option, you report an adjustment under the *alternative minimum tax* (AMT). The adjustment is the same as the amount of compensation income you would report if you had a nonqualified option: the difference between fair market value and the price you paid for the stock. You could pay as much as 28% tax on this amount in the year you exercise your option. Under some complicated rules, you may recover most or all of this payment in the year you sell the stock. Planning for the AMT can be an intricate and painful process.

Employee Stock Purchase Plans

Some employers have broad-based plans permitting employees to purchase stock, often at a discount of 15% from the current value. If you participate in one of these plans, you won't report income until you sell the stock. At that time, you may have to report a portion of the sale price as compensation income rather than capital gain.

Chapter 3
Stock 101

What is stock? For some people, equity compensation is the first experience with owning stock. Even if you've previously owned or traded stock, you may not have a clear idea what you owned. This chapter explains what stock is, and also tells how to buy and sell stock.

What Is a Corporation?

Begin by thinking about what a *corporation* is. Any answer to that question is necessarily abstract, because a corporation isn't something you can see or touch. It doesn't physically exist. That's why people sometimes say a corporation is a *legal fiction*. That doesn't mean corporations aren't real. It just means their reality is . . . intangible.

The abstraction we call a corporation is a way of organizing the legal rights of people connected with a business enterprise. Here's a brief summary of the chief characteristics:

- Day-to-day management of the corporation is vested in the *officers*, and other people who work under the direction of the officers.

- The *board of directors* makes major policy decisions (often including adoption and administration of equity compensation arrangements), and has authority to appoint and remove officers.

- *Shareholders* vote on major decisions (often including approval of equity compensation arrangements adopted by the board of directors) and elect the directors.

Owning Stock

When you acquire stock, you're becoming a shareholder—the ultimate boss of the corporation. But you didn't work so hard for those shares just so you could vote for the directors. Shares of stock also represent economic ownership. The shareholders own the company. That's why stock has value.

Even at this level, though, things are pretty abstract. As a shareholder you have two economic rights: (1) the right to receive dividends, when and if the directors declare them, and (2) the right to receive a share of the liquidation proceeds if the company goes out of business. Yet many stocks are quite valuable even though they pay no dividends and the company's unlikely to liquidate at any time in the foreseeable future. That's OK: if the company has *assets*, and more importantly, a steady and rising stream of *earnings*, the market will recognize the value of the company in the price of its stock.

You should be aware that the price of a company's stock can plummet, sometimes for reasons outside the company's control. Every year, many corporations fail, leaving their shareholders with worthless stock. In the aggregate, though, stocks provide such a good investment that you almost *have* to own some if you want to be a successful investor, as explained in Chapter 7.

Stock Certificates

You may have seen, or even personally own, stock certificates. These are pieces of paper that document your ownership of one or more shares. Most often, when people buy and sell stocks through a broker, they never see the certificates. They simply get a statement from the broker saying that they own a certain number of shares. You don't need to have a certificate to be a shareholder. You may receive certificates in connection with your equity compensation, but it's also possible you'll own shares without ever receiving certificates.

Buying and Selling Shares

When you buy shares under a plan offered by your company, you have to follow the procedures set forth in the plan or in your option agreement. Many plans also provide a way for you to sell shares, too. It's possible, though, that you'll find yourself with stock certificates and not know how to sell them.

In this case, you need to establish an account with a stock broker. This may seem like an unfamiliar and even somewhat scary thing to do. In reality, nothing could be simpler. Brokers *love* to have people open new accounts, so they'll make it very easy for you to do so. It's pretty much like opening a bank account. You fill out some forms, including one that gives your social security number. You also give them some money—or some stock. They'll tell you the rest, including how you give an order to buy or sell stock.

If the only thing you need to do is sell the shares and get your hands on the money, you may as well go to a discount broker with a convenient office. Give more thought to your choice if you plan to continue using the brokerage account. Consider whether you need the kind of guidance and hand-holding you get from a full-service broker (where fees are higher), or whether you want to be able to use your computer to buy and sell stocks over the Internet. There are many brokers to choose from, and no single one is right for everyone.

Chapter 4
Income Tax 101

Many people pay income tax without understanding much about it. I often run into people, for example, who know that *deductions* are good, and *credits* are good, but don't have a clear idea of the difference between the two. To think intelligently about your equity compensation you need to understand the basic structure of the income tax—and also understand what your *tax bracket* is. Fortunately, these basics are quite simple.

Four Steps

Figuring your income tax involves four steps:

1. Find your *total income*.

2. Subtract your deductions: the result is your *taxable income*.

3. Apply the tax rates to find your tax.

4. Subtract your withholding and other payments and credits: the result is the tax you owe, or the refund you have coming.

Step 1: Total Income

The first step is to add up your *total income*. Total income includes many kinds of receipts: wages, interest, dividends, business and partnership income, amounts you receive from IRAs and pension plans, alimony, lottery winnings—and the list goes on. Of special interest: it includes your profit from sales of assets such as stock or real property—in other words, *capital gain*. But some items aren't included. For example, total income doesn't include inheritances or gifts you receive, or life insurance proceeds.

Step 2: Deductions

The second step in determining your income tax is to subtract the *deductions*. Deductions come in four main flavors:

Business deductions. These deductions are claimed as part of the calculation of business income, so they're actually part of the determination of total income in Step 1. But take note: deductions related to investment activities are *not* considered business deductions.

Adjustments. *Adjustments* are a special class of deductions you're allowed to claim even if you don't claim *itemized deductions* (see below). You claim your adjustments at the bottom of page 1 of Form 1040. Among the items here are your contributions to an IRA or other retirement plan, student loan interest, and alimony you paid. When you subtract your adjustments from total income, you arrive at an important number called *adjusted gross income*. On Form 1040, that's the last number on page 1 and also the number at the top of page 2.

Itemized deductions; standard deduction. Each year you're allowed to claim *itemized deductions* or the *standard deduction*, whichever is larger. Itemized deductions include such items as medical expenses, state and local taxes, mortgage interest and investment expenses. If those items don't add up to a large enough total, you claim the standard deduction instead. Your standard deduction depends on your filing status and is adjusted each year for inflation. Most people find that the standard deduction is larger than the total of their itemized deductions—at least, before they become homeowners. As your income grows, you're likely to see your itemized deductions grow also. When they become large enough, you should claim itemized deductions instead of the standard deduction.

> For a single filer in 2000 (not blind or over age 65) the standard deduction is $4,400.

Exemptions. You're allowed a deduction just for being you: a personal exemption. You're also allowed an exemption for each person who qualifies as your *dependent*. Like the standard deduction, the exemption deduction is adjusted each year for inflation.

> The personal exemption amount for 2000 is $2,800.

Taxable income. When you've subtracted all of these deductions from your total income, the result is your *taxable income*.

Step 3: Apply the Tax Rates

Once you know your taxable income, you apply the tax rates to find out your tax. Most people do this quite simply by looking up their taxable income in a table supplied with their tax form. If your income includes long-term capital gain, you have to perform a special calculation to obtain the benefit of the lower rate that applies to this type of income.

Step 4: Subtract Payments and Credits

The tax law allows you to claim certain *credits* that reduce the amount of tax you owe. For example, if you pay for child care, a portion of that expense may be allowed as a credit. And of course, you get credit for any tax you've already paid—including income tax your employer withheld from your paycheck and any estimated tax payments you made during the year. Subtract your credits and payments from your tax to find out how much you owe. If your payments exceed the tax, you're in luck: you have a refund coming!

Note that deductions and credits have very different effects on your tax. A deduction reduces your taxable income, before you apply the tax rates. That means a $100 deduction doesn't reduce your taxes by $100. If you're in the 28 percent tax bracket, a $100 deduction reduces your taxes by $28. A credit, on the other hand, reduces your tax directly. A $100 credit reduces your tax by $100.

Your Tax Bracket

Apart from knowing the basic structure of the income tax, there's one other basic concept you need to understand: your *tax bracket.* Knowing your tax bracket can help with your tax planning, because it tells you approximately how much value you'll get from a deduction, and also how much added tax you'll pay if you have additional income. Nearly everyone has heard of tax brackets and has a vague understanding of what they are, but there are widespread misconceptions about the precise concept.

Remember that Step 3 above involves applying the tax rates to your taxable income. Here's what really goes on. There are a series of tax rates, with the lowest being 15% and the highest being 39.6%. When you apply the tax rates, you're applying the lowest rate to your first chunk of taxable income, the next higher rate to the next chunk of taxable income, and so on. For example, a single filer in 1999 with taxable income of $50,000 will pay tax at the rate of 15% on the first $25,750 of taxable income, and 28% on the rest. This isn't enough taxable income to reach the next tax rate, which is 31%.

Notice that in this example roughly half of the income is taxed at 15% and half at 28%. That means the blended rate is roughly halfway between those two rates, or about 21.5%. But this person's *tax bracket* is 28%. Adding $1,000 to her income will increase her tax by $280; similarly, a $1,000 deduction will *decrease* her tax by $280.

Misconceptions. One of the misconceptions about tax brackets is that you may suffer some whopping hit of additional tax when you move into the next higher bracket. That doesn't happen. If your income is right at the top of the 28% bracket and you earn another $100 of income, you move into the 31% bracket. But all that means is you pay $31 of tax on that $100 of added income. You still pay 15% on your first dollars of income and 28% on the income after that.

Another misconception is that your tax bracket somehow attaches to your normal amount of earnings, so that other types of income don't affect it. For example, suppose your normal earnings put you in the 28% bracket. Then you have some extraordinary added amount of income—perhaps you converted a traditional IRA to a Roth IRA, or had a large short-term capital gain. You don't *own* the 28% bracket. If your added income is large enough to cause you to pay tax at a higher rate, then it moves you into that higher bracket, at least for that year.

> Long-term capital gains won't move your other income into a higher bracket. In tax lingo, we say these gains, which are taxed at special, favorable rates, are "stacked on top of" ordinary income.

There's yet another misconception about tax brackets. Some people try to relate their tax bracket to the amount of tax withheld from their paychecks. But the withholding rate doesn't correspond to your tax bracket. Recall the example above where the *blended* rate of tax was around 21.5%. Withholding rates are designed to hit your blended rate, not your tax bracket. The actual amount withheld depends on your income level, the number of allowances you claimed, and certain other factors. If you're in the 28% bracket, adding $1,000 to your earnings will add $280 to your tax, but the amount added to your withholding may be somewhat larger or smaller.

Determining your tax bracket. Even if you prepare your own income tax return, you may not know what your tax bracket is because most people determine their tax by looking it up in a table that says, for example, if your taxable income is between $40,000 and $40,050, your tax is $7,912 (single filer, 1998). You can tell by eyeballing those numbers that the blended rate is about 20% (or I can, anyway, because I see that $7,912 is close to $8,000, which is 20% of $40,000). But that doesn't tell you your tax bracket.

There are two ways to find your tax bracket. One is to look at that same table and see how much higher your tax would be if your income increased by $100. But there's a better way, and that is to look at the *tax rate schedules* that come in the instructions to Form 1040. Find the amount of *taxable income* on your tax return (income after all deductions) and see where it fits in the tax rate schedule for your filing status. Looking at the tax rate schedule is helpful because it tells you how close you are to moving into the next tax bracket. For example, if your taxable income places you in the 31% bracket, but just a few hundred dollars short of the 36% bracket, you know that a $20,000 bonus will be taxed mostly at 36%, even though your tax bracket before you receive the bonus is 31%.

Marginal rate. People sometimes refer to *marginal rate* as a synonym for tax bracket. Others use this term for a more precise concept. If you're in the 31% tax bracket, an added $100 of income won't necessarily result in $31 of extra tax. The added income may cause you to lose out on some deduction or credit you would otherwise claim, so the real tax cost of that $100 may be greater than $31. In situations where precision is important, you need to know your exact marginal rate, not your tax bracket. But you can only learn that through examining (or recalculating) your entire income tax return.

Chapter 5
Capital Gains 101

Most forms of equity compensation present the possibility that you will have *capital gains*. Even if you've never had capital gains before, you probably have at least a vague sense that they get special tax treatment, with a favorable tax rate. It's helpful to understand how the rules for capital gains and losses can help you—or hurt you.

Two Basic Flavors

All of the income and deductions you may have are divided into two categories: *ordinary* income and loss, and *capital* gain and loss. Ordinary income includes your wages, of course, and also includes many other types of income: interest, dividends, pension and IRA distributions, alimony income—the list goes on, because it includes everything *other than* capital gain.

So what is capital gain? Generally speaking, you have capital gain or loss when you sell a *capital asset*, which is basically anything of lasting value, other than something you sell as inventory to customers.

We'll see that equity compensation can result in ordinary income, capital gain, or some of both. In some cases, the amount of income you have from ordinary income rather than capital gain depends on when you exercise an option, or how long you hold your stock, or even whether you make a special filing with the IRS called a *section 83b election*.

Tax Treatment of Capital Gains

The most significant difference between capital gain and ordinary income is the tax rate for *long-term* capital gain.

This is capital gain from an asset you held more than a year: at least a year and a day. If you have a long-term capital gain that isn't wiped out by a capital loss, you pay tax on that gain at the rate of 20% (or 10%, to the extent the gain falls in what would be the 15% bracket for ordinary income).

That's a huge difference. Most people who have capital gains would otherwise pay tax at rates between 28% and 39.6%. Compared to those numbers, a 20% rate is *sweet*. And if you're in the 15% bracket, the ability to pay only 10% on your long-term capital gain is like getting a one-third off "sale price" on your taxes.

You may also have *short-term* capital gains. These are gains from sale of an asset you held one year or less. Notice that if you sell stock on the anniversary of the date you acquired it, your gain or loss is short-term. You need to hold one more day to get long-term gain or loss.

Short-term capital gain is taxed at the same rates as ordinary income. No special tax break there. But short-term capital gain can still be better than ordinary income. That's because of the way the tax law treats capital *losses*.

Tax Treatment of Capital Losses

Special rules apply to capital losses. Just like capital gains, you have to divide them between long-term and short-term. Then you apply them in the following order:

- First, deduct the loss against capital gains in the same category (long-term loss against long-term gain, short-term loss against short-term gain).

- Next, if the capital loss in one category is larger than the amount of capital gain in that category, deduct the loss against any gain that's left in the other category (long-term loss against short-term gain, or short-term loss against long-term gain).

- If you still have some capital loss left after these two steps, apply the loss against your ordinary income—but only up to $3,000 of capital loss.

- Any remaining amount of capital loss *carries over* to the next year, when you can use it just as if it was a brand-new loss for that year. If you still don't use all of it, you carry it to the next year, and so on.

Generally speaking, an *ordinary* deduction or loss is better than a capital loss. If you have an ordinary loss of $5,000, you don't have to worry about a $3,000 limit, and the loss will reduce your ordinary income. A *capital* loss will reduce your capital gain—the part of your income that may be taxed at a lower rate. Worse, if your capital loss is large enough, you may have to carry part of it to the next year, rather than using all of it to save taxes right away.

Basis

You don't know capital gains until you understand *basis*. Some people have a hard time with this concept, so don't worry if it doesn't seem obvious to you. The basic idea is that basis represents your investment in a particular asset.

For a simple example, suppose you buy 100 shares of stock through a broker. The stock is trading at $25, so you pay $2,500. On top of that you pay a $30 commission to the broker. Your *basis* for the stock is $2,530, ($25.30 per share) because that's what it cost to buy it.

There are many rules for determining basis in different situations, but most of them follow a fairly simple logic. For example, suppose the stock you bought in the previous example split two for one. Now you have 200 shares where you had 100 before. You didn't pay any additional money to acquire these shares, so your investment didn't increase. Your total basis stays the same, at $2,530, and your basis per share is now $12.65.

Basis includes reported income. There's one rule of particular importance when it comes to equity compensation. Generally, if you have to report income when you receive property, your basis includes the amount of income you reported. For example, if your employer grants stock to you worth $5,000, you'll report $5,000 of income—and you'll own the stock with a basis of $5,000. If you sell it for $5,600, you'll report a gain of $600, even though you never actually paid for the stock. It's as if your employer paid you $5,000 in cash and you used the money to buy the stock.

Amount realized. When you sell stock or other capital assets, you report gain or loss based on the difference between the *amount realized* and your basis. The amount realized is what you received for the sale, including any debts that attached to the property. If you sell stock through a broker, the amount realized is the selling price of the stock minus the brokerage commission and any other expenses of sale.

Form 1099-B. When you sell stock through a broker, you'll receive a form that indicates the amount realized. Some people panic when they see *Form 1099-B* because it reports the entire amount realized, not just the *gain*. You may hold stock with a basis of $7,000 and sell it for $9,000 for a $2,000 gain. The form you get from the broker simply says you sold for $9,000. It's up to you to determine your basis and correctly report the gain or loss on your tax return.

Capital Gain Planning

Planning for capital gains can run into complexities that test the patience of even the most capable tax advisor. Yet anyone who holds capital assets can be aware of basic capital gain planning techniques. Tax planning shouldn't dictate your handling of capital assets in all cases, but you should take these points into account in making your decisions.

Avoid Short-Term Gains. Short-term capital gains are taxed at the same rates as ordinary income, while long-term capital gains receive favorable treatment. Generally speaking, you have it within your power to convert short-term capital gains into long-term capital gains, through the simple expedient of postponing sales. If you're selling at a gain, try to avoid selling shares you've held a year or less.

Of course there are situations where it's necessary or desirable to sell before your stock is long-term. There are also situations where it doesn't make a difference whether you hold long-term; for example, where you have a large capital loss that will swallow up all your gains, long-term and short-term.

Sometimes you have to choose between selling a short-term asset with a small gain and a long-term asset with a large gain. Selling the long-term asset will give you a lower rate, but the short-term asset will give you a smaller gain. There's no rule of thumb for resolving this conflict: you have to weigh the costs of each choice based on the particular facts of the situation.

Deferral. That's a boring word for a mundane concept: other things being equal, it's better to pay taxes later rather than sooner. The most obvious way to accomplish this is simply to avoid selling your winners. Even after your gains are long-term, it pays to delay sale—and taxes—from one year to the next. Wait until next year to sell and, if possible, the year after that. The sooner you sell your winners, the sooner Uncle Sam takes his bite.

This strategy is consistent with a tried and true investment strategy for accumulating wealth: buy and hold. People who sit on their stocks for long periods of time generally make out better than those who buy and sell frequently. But there are times when it's important to sell holdings, particularly to achieve diversification, as explained in Chapter 7.

Minimize gains. If you must sell a capital asset, it's usually best to minimize gains by selling assets with the highest basis. For example, you may have shares you acquired a long time ago for $15 and shares you acquired 18 months ago for $25. You're planning to sell some shares now at the current price of $30. With a little care, you can arrange to sell the newer shares and report a smaller gain. To do this, you may have to *identify* the shares you're selling, as explained in Chapter 43.

Avoid long-term losses. This rule of thumb goes against the grain of the buy-and-hold theory of investing. If you hold stock that has declined in value, you shouldn't rush to sell it simply to prevent the loss from becoming a long-term loss. Yet there are situations where a short-term loss is much better than a long-term loss.

For example, suppose you have plenty of capital gains, both short-term and long-term. You're planning to sell your XYZ stock, which is now trading at a $5,000 loss. If you sell while the loss is short-term, the loss will reduce your short-term gain, which is taxed at ordinary income tax rates. If you wait until the loss is long-term, it will reduce your long-term capital gain. In this situation, the short-term loss can save you as much as 39.6%, or nearly $2,000, while the long-term loss saves you $1,000 at best.

Use large losses to soak up gains. If you have a large loss in one year, and also have stocks with gains, you don't have to worry about selling the gains right away because any unused loss will carry over to the next year. But suppose you're in the opposite situation. You have a large gain in one year, and stocks with large losses. In this situation, it may be to your advantage to sell the losing stock. The reason: capital losses carry *forward* but not *back*. You could end up paying tax on a large gain in Year 1, and be stuck with a large loss in some later year that you can't fully use because of the $3,000 limitation.

Protect long-term gains. Except in the situation described in the previous paragraph, it can be an advantage to prevent capital losses from reducing your long-term gains. You get more bang for your buck on a capital loss if it can be used against short-term gains or ordinary income rather than against your long-term gains. If you have a choice as to which year to sell losing stock and report a loss, it may be better to choose a year when you don't have long-term gains—unless the loss is so large it will otherwise go unused.

Chapter 6
Gift and Estate Tax 101

Equity compensation can result in wealth you never had before. As part of your personal financial planning, you should think about how it affects your estate plan. This isn't a do-it-yourself topic: estate planning should be done in consultation with a qualified professional. It helps if you know the basic rules of the game, though.

Gifts and Income Tax

Before we turn to gift and estate tax, let's take a look at how gifts affect your income tax.

Recipient doesn't report income. Gifts you receive aren't considered income. You don't report them on your income tax return in any way. There are two important qualifications on this simple rule.

- **True gifts.** This rule applies only to true gifts. You can't avoid paying income tax by calling something a gift when it isn't. For example, a "gift" you receive in exchange for services or some other consideration isn't a gift.

- **Income after gift.** If you receive a gift of property that produces income, you must report any income produced after the gift. For example, if you receive stock as a gift, you must report any dividends paid on that stock after the gift. There's an important exception for gifts of nonqualified options, described in Chapter 17.

No deduction except for charitable gifts. Some people hear that you can give $10,000 to a child "tax-free" and wonder if this means they can claim a deduction for such gifts. I'm afraid the answer is no. There is no deduction for gifts—except gifts to qualifying charities. The $10,000 limit applies to a *gift tax* exemption that's explained below. It has nothing to do with your *income tax*.

Basis and holding period. If the gift consists of property other than cash, the basis and holding period of the property will transfer to the recipient. It's important for the recipient to know when the donor acquired the property, the cost of the property, and any other information that would affect the property's basis. Ideally, the recipient of the gift should also receive records that will provide adequate proof of these facts.

It's also necessary to know the *value* of the property at the time of the gift. As donor, you need this information to determine whether the gift exceeds the $10,000 exclusion and, if so, the amount to report on the gift tax return. The recipient of the gift may also need this information to determine whether a deduction is available if the property is later sold at a loss.

Special rule for losses. If the property already had a loss at the time of the gift, the person receiving the gift can't deduct that loss on a later sale. Any loss deduction is limited to the amount the stock went down *after* the date of the gift. But for sales at a gain, the recipient can use the donor's basis.

Example: You bought stock for $10,000 and later gave it to your child when its value was $9,000. That means a $1,000 loss was "built-in" at the time of the gift. Your basis in the stock transfers to your child, but only for sales at a gain. If your child sells the stock for $8,500, the loss is only $500, even though you would have been able to deduct $1,500 if *you* had sold the stock. If your child sells the stock for $10,700, though, the gain is only $700, even though the stock went up $1,700 while your child held it. If your child sells the stock for a price between $9,000 (the value at the time of the gift) and $10,000 (the transferred basis), there is no gain or loss on the sale.

The holding period transfers, too. That means that if you held stock for more than a year before the gift, any sale by the recipient will produce long-term capital gain or loss—even if the recipient holds the stock for only a single day.

The Unified Transfer Tax

Federal estate and gift tax work hand in hand. Gifts you make during your lifetime can affect the amount of estate tax that's owed at your death.

To understand this, begin with the estate tax. This tax generally doesn't kick in until you leave more than $675,000 to someone other than your spouse or a charity. (The $675,000 figure applies to 2000. That amount is scheduled to increase to $1,000,000 over the next several years.) The way this works is there is a *credit* that applies against the estate tax, to wipe out the tax that would otherwise apply to the first $675,000 of taxable estate.

This same credit is used against the gift tax. If you make a taxable gift, you don't actually pay tax on the gift unless the total amount of gifts in your lifetime is greater than $675,000. Because the same credit is used for both taxes—it's actually called the *unified credit*—any part of the credit that gets used up because of taxable gifts will reduce the amount of credit that's available for your estate when you die.

For wealthier individuals, it often makes sense to use the unified credit during their lifetime. But you don't want to use it unnecessarily if you think there's any chance your taxable estate will be more the $675,000. That's where the $10,000 gift exclusion comes in.

Gifts Under $10,000

Under the gift tax you can give $10,000 per donee per year without reporting a taxable gift. If you're married, you and your spouse can jointly give $20,000 per donee per year, even if the entire gift comes from just one of you.

(To do this, you and your spouse must file gift tax returns and elect "gift-splitting.") You can use this rule to remove a large dollar amount of assets from your estate without incurring any gift tax or reducing your unified credit.

> **Example:** Suppose you're married and have three adult children, each of whom is married. Each year, you can give $20,000 to each child, and the spouse of each child, for total gifts of $120,000 per year without any gift tax implications.

This exclusion applies only to gifts of *present interests*. If you want to make your gift through a trust, you need to have an expert make certain the trust contains provisions that will prevent your gift from being a *future interest*. You can also make gifts of present interests through a Uniform Transfers to Minors Account, but these accounts are not well suited to transfers of large dollar amounts for various reasons, including potentially adverse estate tax consequences.

Other Exclusions

The $10,000 exclusion isn't the only way to make gifts without incurring gift tax. There's an unlimited exclusion for gifts to your spouse. (A $100,000 limit applies if your spouse is not a United States citizen.) There's also an unlimited exclusion for the payment of medical expenses or educational costs, provided you make these payments directly to the service provider or educational institution.

Estate Planning

Estate planning is an exact science and a major industry. Even if you don't think you have to worry about estate tax, it's important to make certain your assets will pass in the way you intend, and avoid unnecessary probate costs. If there's a possibility the estate tax will apply—in many places, the cost of a good home and a reasonable life insurance policy will get you more than halfway there—it's important to see what can be done to prevent overpaying Uncle Sam. Estate tax rates are very high, and it's very often possible to save tens of thousands, or even hundreds of thousands, with some relatively inexpensive trust arrangements and other planning techniques.

Chapter 7
Investing 101

Whether you receive options or stock, your equity compensation is an *investment*. A knowledge of basic investment principles will help you manage this asset for maximum advantage.

In connection with my work on the *Tax Guide for Investors* (www.fairmark.com), I read many books and other publications about investing. One thing that strikes me in all this reading is how simple the most important concepts are. There's a mystique about investing, and no end to the knowledge and creativity that can apply to the subject. But you don't need years of study to be a successful investor. The basics can be set forth in just 11 words: start early, pay debts, buy stocks, diversify, avoid churning, control expenses.

Start Early

Experts agree on what is the single most important thing in determining how successful you will be as an investor. It isn't stock picking, or predicting the market's direction. It isn't your ability to read a balance sheet or engage in fancy trading transactions. It's simply this: *how early you start.*

The earlier you start investing, the more successful you'll be. The reason is the phenomenal mathematical power of compound interest. The earlier you start saving and investing, the more wealth you'll accumulate, and the less overall effort you'll have to put into accumulating that wealth. Your money will be doing the work instead of you.

Let's take a simple example. Suppose you have an investment that compounds at the rate of 8% per year—

roughly the historical average rate of growth of the stock market, after taking inflation into account. You put $50 per month into this investment for a period of 30 years. At the end of that time you've put away $18,000, and investment earnings have caused it to grow to $75,000.

Now suppose you start 10 years later and save twice as much per month. After 20 years of saving $100 per month you've put away $24,000 and earnings bring your account to a little less than $60,000. The earlier start required $6,000 less in savings and produced an account that was $15,000 larger.

The point is not to make you kick yourself for not starting sooner. Most people, myself included, get started on serious savings later than they should. The conclusion is simply that anyone without a serious program of saving and investing should get one going right away. The earlier you start, the easier and more successful it will be.

Pay Debts

Debts are negative investments. They provide a negative return. If investments are a powerful way to build wealth, what do you suppose a negative investment is? This isn't the place for a long lecture on paying off your credit cards, but a list of the key pieces of investment wisdom wouldn't be complete without this observation.

Buy Stocks

Buy stocks! Peter Lynch offers that terse bit of advice, and so do virtually all investment writers I've read, including Jonathan Clements of the *Wall Street Journal*, Charles Schwab in his excellent book on investing, the witty and commonsensical Andrew Tobias, the ubiquitous Suze Orman, those rowdy iconoclasts David and Tom Gardner of *Motley Fool* fame, and the even rowdier Jonathan Hoenig, author of *Greed is Good*. (See *Resources* in the appendix for descriptions of some of these books). What's the big deal? Are these folks simply into stocks? Why not other investments?

Historically, stocks have proven to be the most rewarding investment you can make. Better than bonds or real estate, better than precious metals or collectibles. The reason is simple: companies *grow*. Bonds don't grow, and neither do real estate or commodities. Successful companies grow, and when they do, their shareholders prosper. This isn't mere theory. Over short periods of time, other investments sometimes outpace stocks, but over the long haul stocks have proved to be by far the best way to accumulate wealth.

There are various ways to buy stocks. You don't necessarily have to open a brokerage account, although that could be a good move. You can buy stocks by investing in mutual funds, or by making sure the bulk of your 401k account is in stocks.

Some people feel that investing in stocks is too risky. That may be true if you're investing for a relatively short period of time. It wouldn't make sense to have all your money in stocks if you're saving for a down payment on a home next year. Over the longer term, though, the greater risk is that you will achieve inadequate returns from other investments. So one of the keys to successful investing is to buy stocks.

I'm not suggesting that stocks should be your only investment. Other types of investments have their merits. You need to have some of your money held in a form that can be reduced to cash on short notice without damaging your long-term investment strategy. And it makes sense to hold some investments that hedge against the possibility of a significant drop in the stock market. The problem is that many people hold far less of their investments in stock than they should. The likely result is that they will have inferior investment returns in the long run.

Diversify

That's a fancy word for a simple concept: don't keep all your eggs in one basket. If you own just one stock, or if one stock is a very high percentage of your overall net worth, you run the risk of suffering major losses. Even very good companies sometimes have reverses that drastically reduce their value. It's true that the stock market as a whole sometimes goes down, sometimes by significant amounts, but the stock market as a whole has always bounced back to ever higher levels. The same can't be said of individual companies.

At the very least, you need to own several stocks in different industries. Many experts advise much broader diversification than this by investing in mutual funds, especially those that broadly index the stock market. Even investing in one of the popular funds that index the S&P 500 may not be broad enough according to some, because these funds are dominated by a handful of the largest stocks within them. Consider putting some of your investment dollars in a fund that attempts to mimic an even broader index.

Diversification is a particular issue for people who receive equity compensation. The good news with this form of compensation is that in some cases it can grow so much that it becomes a large part of your net worth. The bad news is that no matter how sound the company is, it isn't healthy to have all or nearly all of your net worth in a single company. If you reach the point where it would be a devastating blow for your finances if your equity compensation declined in value, you should be thinking about how to diversify your holdings.

Avoid Churning

Apart from starting early and investing in stocks, probably the most important piece of investment advice is to avoid jumping in and out of stocks or mutual funds. Frequent selling, or *churning*, is a chief source of poor investment performance. Investors who have the patience to hold on for the long term almost invariably do better than those who sell frequently.

One reason is that churning can be expensive. When you buy and sell stocks, you incur brokerage commissions on both the purchase and the sale. If the stock has gone up, you pay tax on your gain. You also incur a hidden expense called the *bid-ask spread*. This is the difference between what a seller is willing to receive for the stock (the asking price, or *ask*) and what the buyer is willing to pay for the stock (the *bid*). To buy stock, you have to pay the asking price, and when you sell it you get the bid price. The gap between these (and sometimes more, depending on how successful your broker is in getting the best possible price) disappears into the pockets of the market makers, and is often a much higher cost than the brokerage commissions. If this sounds mysterious, just take my word for this: trading in and out of stocks can be a lot more expensive than it looks.

There's another problem with trading in and out of stocks. Almost of necessity, you're more likely to be wrong than right when you decide on the direction of a particular stock or the market as a whole. That's part of the way the market works.

Don't believe me? Try this thought experiment. You've seen stock charts with the zigs and zags. Sometimes they go up dramatically for a long period of time and then drop just as dramatically. Imagine such a chart, with a big upswing, then a big drop and another upswing.

Now mentally place your hand over the part of the chart that appears after the big upswing. All the chart shows is a stock (or market) that's zooming to the moon. No one knows about the big drop that's in store. What do you suppose people were saying about that stock or market at that point in time? The likelihood is that people were positively euphoric about the rise. People weren't selling; they were buying like mad to get in on the profits of this tremendous rise. The greatest amount of buying was happening just at the wrong time, when the stock was about to run out of steam.

Now move your hand so that the big drop is visible, but the subsequent rise is still hidden. What were people saying then? The stock is a dog—worse, it's a dog with fleas. You must be crazy to hold that stock. Get out and cut your losses! Most people will be wrong again, selling just when the stock is preparing to rise.

This basic insight about stocks—that most people are buying precisely when they should be selling and selling when they should be buying—leads some people to believe they should adopt a contrarian approach: buy when things look gloomy, and sell at the time of greatest optimism. This approach is fraught with risk, though. Try moving your hand to the *middle* of one of the ups or downs to see why this is so. You may be buying at a time that looks gloomy (and therefore seemingly a good time for the stock to turn around and rise) only to find that things *really are* gloomy for this stock, and it still has a long way to fall before it reaches the bottom. Trading against the trend can be hazardous to your financial health.

Fortunately there's a simple answer to the dilemma. Buy a diversified portfolio of quality stocks (directly or through mutual funds) and hold them. Don't try to guess which way the market will move. Don't panic when it falls: remember that it will rise again. Don't kick yourself for failing to sell at the peak because this is something that even the most brilliant minds in investing are unable to do on a regular basis. In fact, the best thing may be to simply forget you have these investments. There are times when it's important to sell an investment, but far more investors make mistakes in selling too early than in selling too late.

Control Expenses

The name of the game in investing is to maximize your return over the long haul. Expenses just eat away at your return. It's important to control expenses. Here are some things to look out for.

- **Costs of trading.** I covered this above, but mention it here again because it's a key reason for inferior investment results.

- **Margin interest.** Borrowing to buy stocks creates what we call *leverage*. That means you can have greater gains than would otherwise be possible—

and also greater losses. Margin interest is the price you pay for the privilege of incurring this greater risk.

- **Loads and other mutual fund expenses.** Mutual funds vary widely in their expense levels. Some keep their expenses very low, so that nearly all of the investment return they generate ends up in your account. Others have much higher expenses that create a significant drag on your overall return. Most painful of all are those that have high sales charges, or *loads*. Avoid these funds unless you are receiving valuable investment advice from the person who is putting you into the fund and generating a handsome commission from your money.

- **Taxes.** The single largest investment expense is taxes, so anything you can do to control that expense will be to your significant advantage. Much of this book is about tax planning in one sense or another. For much more on the subject of investment taxation, visit the *Tax Guide for Investors* at www.fairmark.com.

On our web site at **www.fairmark.com** you'll find updates to the material in this book and a message board where you can ask questions or post comments.

Part II
Stock Grants and Purchases

Most companies that provide equity compensation offer it in the form of *stock options*, or participation in an *employee stock purchase plan* (also called a *section 423 plan*). These types of equity compensation are covered in later parts of this book. In this part we look at the rules that apply when you acquire stock from your company *without* such arrangements.

Chapter 8 provides some terminology you need to get started. In Chapter 9 we look at rules that apply when you receive a stock grant or award from your company, or buy stock from the company. Rules explained in other parts of this book are based on rules in this chapter. Turn to Chapter 10 for planning ideas.

The tax rules for stock options are based on the rules described in these chapters. A quick skim of this part of the book may be helpful even if your compensation is in the form of options.

Part II
Stock Grants and Purchases

Chapter 8
Terminology for Stock Grants and Purchases

You need to know some tax lingo before you can read about stock grants and purchases. Here are the basic terms:

Stock grants and awards. If your company gives you stock without requiring payment from you (other than withholding), you've received a *stock grant*, also called a *stock award*. Other terms sometimes used include *restricted* stock and *founder's* stock.

Vested or not vested. Sometimes a company grants stock with no strings attached. You can sell the stock or keep it, and you don't give anything up if you stop working for the company. On the other hand, the company may insist that you earn the right to keep the stock. For example, the company may say that if you stop working for the company within a specified period, you forfeit the stock, or you have to sell it back to the company for the amount you originally paid.

These conditions can affect the tax consequences of receiving a stock grant, or buying stock from your company. We have one set of rules for when the stock is *vested*, and another for when the stock is *not vested*. Generally, your stock is *vested* if you can sell it, or if you can keep the stock (or at least get full value for it) when you stop working for the company. If both conditions are absent (in other words, you can't sell the stock, and you'll either forfeit it or sell it back for less than full value if you leave your job), the stock is *not vested*.

Example: Your company grants you 500 shares of stock, but you'll forfeit the stock if you stop working for the company within the next year. The stock isn't *vested* until the year is up.

For most purposes you're the owner of the stock even before it's vested. For example, unless you've agreed otherwise, you have the right to vote as a shareholder and to receive any dividends that are declared and paid during that period. As you'll see in the following chapters, the tax law treats you as if you don't own the stock until it vests, unless you file the *section 83b election*, described below.

Substantial risk of forfeiture. If the company imposes conditions that prevent your stock from being vested, the stock is *subject to a substantial risk of forfeiture.* That's quite a mouthful, and all it means is that the stock isn't vested, so I try to avoid using this term. I mention it here in case you see it somewhere else and wonder where it fits in.

Section 83b election. When you receive stock that isn't vested, you can actually choose which of two sets of tax rules will apply to you. One set of tax rules applies if you do nothing, and a different set of rules applies if you file a *section 83b election.* This is a statement you file with the IRS *within 30 days after you receive the stock* saying that you want the alternate set of tax rules to apply. The following chapters explain the effects of this election.

You can find more details concerning vesting and the section 83b election in Part VIII.

Chapter 9
Rules for Stock Grants and Purchases

This is the most important chapter of this book. It lays the foundation for nearly everything else we discuss: non-qualified options, incentive stock options and employee stock purchase plans. We'll refer back to this chapter when we cover those topics. For now, however, we're concerned only with simple transactions where your company either sells stock to you (at full value or at a bargain price), or gives you a stock grant or award.

> **Tax trap alert.** You may not think you need to worry about the tax consequences if you pay full value for stock you receive from your company. Think again. If the stock isn't vested at the time of purchase, your failure to make a section 83b election, as explained later, could be costly.

Stock grants and stock purchases. We can cover the tax treatment of stock grants and stock purchases together because the rules are exactly the same. You can think of a stock grant as a purchase for zero dollars. Whenever we refer to the amount paid for the stock, that amount is zero in the case of a stock grant or award.

Three sets of rules. There are different rules for each of the following three situations:

- Your stock is *vested* when you receive it.

- Your stock is *not vested* when you receive it.

49

- Your stock is *not vested* when you receive it, and you file the *section 83b election.*

Stock Is Vested

When you receive vested stock, you have to report compensation income for the year you receive it. The amount of income is the fair market value of the stock at the time you received it, reduced by the amount you paid for it, if any.

> **Example:** You receive a stock grant worth $20,000. The stock is vested when you receive it. You have to report $20,000 of compensation income in addition to all your other compensation and non-compensation income for that year.

> **Example:** You buy $20,000 worth of stock from your company for $15,000. The stock is vested when you receive it. You have to report $5,000 of compensation income in addition to all your other compensation and non-compensation income for that year.

See Chapter 40 for guidance on determining fair market value.

> **Cashless income.** Some people tend to associate *income* with *cash.* That isn't the case here. You have to report income, and pay tax, *even if you haven't sold the stock.* You didn't receive any cash—in fact, you may have paid cash to receive the stock—yet you have to come up with money to pay the IRS. Careful planning is essential!
> The amount of tax you'll pay depends on your tax bracket. If the entire amount falls in the 31% bracket in the second example above, you'll pay 31% of $5,000, or $1,550 (plus any social security tax, self-employment tax or state income tax). If your bargain element is large, it's likely that some of the income will push up into a higher tax bracket than your usual one.

No capital gain. You may have capital gain later when you sell the stock. But the income you report now, when you receive the stock, is compensation income, not capital gain. Don't be confused by the fact that your compensation is in the form of stock.

Withholding. If you're an employee, the company is required to withhold on this compensation income. Of course the IRS insists on receiving withholding payments in cash, not in shares of stock. There are various ways the company can handle the withholding requirement. The most common one is simply to require you to pay the withholding amount in cash at the time you exercise the option.

> **Example:** You purchase 1,000 shares of your company's stock for $15 per share when they're worth $40 per share. The stock is vested when you receive it. Your purchase price is $15,000 and your compensation income is $25,000. In addition to the purchase price, the company requires you to pay $9,000 to cover state and federal withholding requirements.

The amount paid must cover federal and state income tax withholding, and the employee share of social security tax as well. The portion that is income tax withholding will be a credit against the tax you owe when you file your return at the end of the year. Be prepared: the amount of withholding won't necessarily be large enough to cover the full amount of the tax due on this income. You may end up owing tax on April 15 even if you paid withholding at the time you exercised the option, because the withholding amount is merely an estimate of the actual tax liability.

> **Example:** You receive a stock grant valued at $10,000 and pay $2,800 in federal withholding. Depending on your tax bracket and other factors, the actual tax on this $10,000 of income may be $3,100 or more, which means you could end up

owing more (or getting a smaller refund) on April 15.

> Withholding you pay when you receive your stock is *not* part of the purchase price. Don't include withholding in your basis when you sell the stock.

Non-employees. If you're not an employee, withholding won't apply when you receive the stock. The income should be reported to you on Form 1099-MISC instead of Form W-2. Remember that this is compensation for services. In general this income will be subject to self-employment tax as well as federal and state income tax.

Tax consequences when you sell the stock. When you sell the stock, you're treated the same as if you had bought it on the date the company gave it to you, for an amount equal to the amount you paid (if any) *plus the amount of income you reported.* Even if you didn't actually pay anything for the stock, you have *basis* equal to the amount of income you reported. It's as if the company paid you that much cash and then you used the cash to buy the stock. If you sell the stock after holding it for a year or less, you'll have a short-term capital gain or loss on the sale. If you hold it for more than a year, your gain or loss will be long-term. It's important to keep a record of when you received the stock, the amount (if any) you paid for it and the amount of income you reported at that time.

Example: You buy 1,000 shares of stock at $20 per share when the value is $50 per share. The stock is vested when you receive it, and you report $30,000 of compensation income. Fifteen months later you sell the stock for $60,000. Your basis includes the $20,000 you paid plus the $30,000 you reported as compensation income. The sale produces a $10,000 long-term capital gain.

Stock Is Not Vested

If the stock isn't vested when you buy it, you have a choice of two different tax treatments. First we'll look at what happens under the general rule. Then we'll see what happens if you file a *section 83b election.*

Under the general rule, receiving stock that isn't vested is a pretty simple event. You report nothing at all at that time. You may *feel* richer if you didn't pay for the stock, or you bought it at a bargain price, but the tax law says you aren't richer until the stock vests. It isn't regular income, or AMT income, or even tax-exempt income. It's nothing at all. Your only obligation at this point is to maintain a record of what stock you acquired, when you received it and the amount (if any) you paid, so you can report the proper consequences on a later sale.

Dividends before vesting. You own the stock while you're waiting for it to vest, so you may receive dividends during this period. Yet the tax law treats you as if you don't own the stock yet, so the company won't report these payments as dividends. Any dividends you receive during this period are treated as *compensation.* The company will report them on your W-2, *not* on Form 1099-DIV.

Tax consequences at vesting. If all goes well, you'll stay with the company long enough to own the stock outright. At that point—when the stock vests—you'll report compensation income equal to the difference between the fair market value of the stock and the amount (if any) you paid for it. In this case, *fair market value is determined on the vesting date.* If the value of the stock goes up while you're waiting for the stock to vest, you'll end up reporting that added value as compensation income when the stock vests.

Example: Your company lets you buy $10,000 worth of stock for $8,000. If your employment terminates within the following two years, you have to sell the stock back to the company for $8,000, the amount you paid. That means your stock isn't vested. You don't file the section 83b election, so you have no income to report in the year of purchase.

Two years later you're still working for the company and the stock vests. At that time the stock is worth $15,000. You report $7,000 of compensation income: the current value of $15,000 minus your cost of $8,000.

The *Alves* trap. You can have a restriction that prevents your stock from being vested even if you pay full value for the stock. Because of a tax case called *Alves*, you may end up paying unnecessary tax in this situation. If the stock goes up in value before it vests, you'll have to report that increase as compensation income at that time. You can avoid this result by filing the section 83b election as explained below.

Tax consequences at sale. A sale of the stock after it's vested will result in capital gain or loss. Your basis will be the amount you paid for the stock plus the amount of income you reported at the time the stock became vested. Your gain or loss will be long-term if you held the stock more than a year after the *vesting date*. Otherwise any gain or loss will be short-term.

Example: Let's continue with the previous example. Six months after the stock vests, you sell it for $20,000. You paid only $8,000 for the stock, but you reported $7,000 of income when the stock vested, so your basis for the stock is $15,000. You report only $5,000 of gain on the sale. Your gain is short-term, even though you held the stock 2½ years, because for tax purposes you're treated as if you acquired the stock on the date it vested.

Tax consequences of forfeiture. It's possible that you'll stop working for the company before the stock vests, and forfeit the stock or have to sell it back for the amount you paid for it—or less. If you sell it back for the same amount you paid to receive the stock, you report no gain or loss. You may feel that you've lost something, because the stock was worth more than you received in the forced sale. But you never included anything in income for that added value, so you can't reduce your income for the loss you suffered. You get no deduction in this situation.

> **Example:** We'll use the previous example one more time. You bought stock worth $10,000 for $8,000, but you reported no income at the time because the stock wasn't vested. Before the stock vested, you left to work for another company and had to sell the stock back for the same $8,000 you originally paid, even though the stock was worth much more. You should report the sale on your tax return, but you have no gain or loss, so it doesn't affect the amount of tax you pay.

If you sell the stock back for *less than* $8,000, you'll report a capital loss.

Section 83b Election

You can change the consequences described above by filing a *section 83b election*. You send a notice to the IRS that includes certain information and declares that you want this election to apply. *This election must be filed within 30 days after you receive the stock.* See Chapter 37 for details on making this election.

If you make the section 83b election, you're treated as if the stock was vested when you receive it:

- You report compensation income at the time you receive the stock, measured by the value of the stock at that time. When you determine the value of the stock for this purpose, you have to ignore the existence of any temporary restriction. If the amount you pay is equal to the fair market value of the stock, the amount of income you report is zero.

- Dividends you receive before the stock vests will *not* be treated as compensation income.

- You have nothing to report at the time the stock vests.

- When you sell the stock, your basis is the amount (if any) you paid for the stock plus the amount of income you reported when you received it. Your holding period goes back to that date, too, so any gain or loss will be long-term if more than a year has elapsed from that date.

By far the biggest problem with the section 83b election is missing the 30-day deadline. You can't wait until you file your tax return to make this election. You have to do it right away.

Tax consequences of forfeiture. It might seem logical to get a deduction if you forfeit stock after making the section 83b election. After all, you voluntarily reported income and paid tax as a result of making this election. A corresponding deduction when you forfeit the stock would make sense. Unfortunately, the law says you can't claim a deduction in this situation. Possibly this rule is designed to prevent people from using the section 83b election to manipulate their income in an artificial way. Whatever the reason, the law is clear: no deduction for a forfeiture.

Before making the section 83b election, be sure you consider the risk that you may forfeit the stock and receive no deduction relative to the income you reported at the time of the election.

Tax consequences of vesting. If you make the section 83b election, there is no tax consequence at the time the stock vests. Under this election you're treated as if the stock was vested when you acquired it, so there is nothing to report at the time it *actually* becomes vested.

Tax consequences at sale. You have the same tax consequences for a sale of stock after a section 83b election as if the stock had been vested when you received it. Your holding period begins on the date you received the stock, and your basis is the amount paid for the stock (if any), increased by the amount of compensation income you reported at that time.

Chapter 10
Planning for Stock Grants and Purchases

Most tax planning for stock grants and purchases revolves around the section 83b election. Even if your company offers stock that will be vested when you receive it, you may wish to consider whether you can change the deal and use the section 83b election to reduce your taxes.

Some of these planning ideas require cooperation from the company. You should bear in mind that good tax planning for you may be bad tax planning for the company. Anything you do to reduce or postpone the amount of compensation income you have to report will cause a corresponding decrease or delay in the amount of compensation deduction the company will enjoy.

Accelerating Income

Suppose you have the following deal with your employer. You'll receive 100 shares of stock without restrictions if your employment continues for another year. This is a simple case of a stock grant without restriction as described in Chapter 9. In some circumstances you can improve on the tax consequences without really changing the deal.

Consider an alternative where you receive the stock *now* instead of having to wait a year—but you'll forfeit the stock if your employment terminates before a year is up. Basically that's the same as the other deal: you get to keep the stock only if you work for that company for a year. You may get a better tax treatment, however, if you make the section 83b election. That would permit you to report compensation income at the time you receive the stock, rather than at the end of the year when the stock vests.

You would do this only if two things are true. First, you expect the value of the stock to go up during that year. There's no point reporting income earlier than necessary just for the sake of paying taxes sooner. If the stock is going up, though, you can use this maneuver to reduce the amount of compensation income you have to report. It may make sense to negotiate this change if you expect a big increase in the stock's value in the near future.

In addition, unless the value of the stock is very small when you receive it, you would want to be pretty confident that your employment will last through the year before heading in this direction. You wouldn't feel smart if you made this change, and paid taxes after filing the section 83b election, only to find that you end up forfeiting the stock.

> **Example:** Your employer offers to reward you with 2,000 shares of stock if you continue to work there another year. You feel that the value of the stock is likely to go up in that time, so you suggest an alternative: you'll receive the stock *now*, but *forfeit* it if you don't continue to work there another year. The company agrees. You receive the stock, make the section 83b election and pay tax on the current value.
>
> Then the unexpected happens. You get an offer you can't refuse from another company. You quit your current job and forfeit the stock. Economically, you're in the same position as if you hadn't made the change, because you wouldn't have received the stock under the original deal. From a tax standpoint though, you're worse off, because you reported income when you made the section 83b election and you won't get any offsetting deduction when you forfeit the stock.

Deferring Income

You can also use the rules for vesting to postpone income. Suppose your company is going to make a stock grant to you, without any restrictions. Normally that would mean you'll report compensation income, but you want to avoid reporting income this year. In this situation you might want to consider *asking* for a restriction on the stock, so that you'll forfeit it if your employment ends within the next year.

Naturally, you would do this only if you're confident that your employment will in fact continue for that period of time. You could be forfeiting a valuable right if you accept such a restriction and you leave your job. In addition, it wouldn't make sense to do this if you anticipate a great increase in the value of the stock while you're waiting for it to vest. These two possibilities—forfeiting the stock or seeing a hefty increase in its value before vesting—make delayed vesting a risky planning device. In limited circumstances, though, it makes sense to at least consider this approach.

You may be tempted to use a very short time period for the stock to vest. For example, if you're going to receive a stock grant in November, you may want to delay vesting until the beginning of January. That's a risky proposition, though. You can delay reporting compensation only if there is a *substantial risk of forfeiture*. The IRS might decide this wasn't *substantial*. There's no specific time period that's safe, but I get nervous with vesting that occurs less than six months after receipt of the stock. Similarly, anything else you do to reduce or eliminate the risk that you'll forfeit the stock may cast doubt on whether the tax deferral will pass muster.

Benefits and Risks of Section 83b Election

The section 83b election can provide multiple benefits. Most obviously, it reduces the amount of compensation income you have to report if the value of your stock goes up during the vesting period. It also starts the clock running sooner for long-term capital gains. This can be to your benefit even if the stock's value doesn't go up during the vesting period, assuming it goes up afterward and you sell it in the year following vesting.

Example: You receive stock with vesting delayed by one year and make the section 83b election. A year later, the value is unchanged, so you didn't avoid any compensation income by making the election. But six months later the stock has gone up and you sell it. Because of the section 83b election, you'll report long-term capital gain. Without the election, your holding period would have started when the stock vested, and you would have had short-term capital gain when you sold the stock.

There's a downside to the election. For one thing, it requires you to pay tax earlier than would otherwise be necessary. All other things being equal, it's better to pay taxes later. And then there's the possibility of a real disaster: paying tax after making the section 83b election and then forfeiting the stock. You didn't just pay tax sooner in this situation. You paid a tax you never would have had to pay at all!

There are some circumstances where you should definitely make the section 83b election. One is where you paid fair market value for the stock, but agreed to have it be subject to a restriction that prevents it from being vested. There's no cost at all to this election, and it can prevent you from having a painful tax bill at the time the stock vests. It's also a good idea to think about the section 83b election in situations where the value of the stock is very low at the time you receive it, and there's a possibility it will rise sharply before vesting. This is often the case when a company is preparing to issue stock in an initial public offering (IPO).

When should you avoid the section 83b election? If the cost of making the election is significant, you have to consider how likely it is that you'll forfeit the stock. If you think there's a good chance you'll leave the company before the stock vests, the section 83b election will be a loser. You can also end up being unhappy with the election if the value of the company's stock goes *down* during the vesting period. In this case, you would pay tax sooner, and also report more income, than if you had not made the election.

Part III
Options in General

This part of the book provides essential information for working with both nonqualified options and incentive stock options. Chapter 11 provides an overview of how options work and introduces you to option terminology. Chapter 12 describes what happens when you receive an option, and what you should do at that time. Chapter 13 explains the difference between nonqualified stock options and incentive stock options, and how to tell the difference between the two. Finally, Chapter 14 takes you step by step through the process of exercising an option.

Part III
Options in General

Chapter 11
Options 101

A stock option is an agreement providing terms under which you can buy a specified number of shares of stock at a specified price. Your option will increase in value as the company's stock grows. If the stock goes down instead, you won't reap value from your option but you won't have lost anything, because you aren't *required* to buy stock. A stock option is that free lunch you've been looking for: a chance to benefit from the upside without any risk of loss on the downside.

Option Terminology

Stock options have their own lingo. Here are the basic terms you need to understand.

- **Grant or award.** You receive the stock option when the company makes a *grant* or *award*.

- **Vesting**. The option agreement or plan may say you can't use the option right away. The time you have to wait before using the option is the *vesting period*. An option is *vested* when you can use the option to buy stock.

- **Exercise.** You *exercise* an option when you notify the company that you want to purchase stock and provide payment according to the terms of the option.

- **Exercise price.** This is the price you pay if you decide to exercise the option. If you have an option to buy 100 shares at $15 per share, your exercise price is $15 per share. The exercise price is also sometimes called the *strike price*, the *striking price* or the *option price*.

- **Spread.** The difference between the current value of the stock and the strike price is the *spread*. If the current value of the stock is $20 and your option permits you to buy it at $15, the spread is $5 per share. The spread is also sometimes called the *bargain element*.

- **In the money.** An option is *in the money* when the spread is positive—in other words, when the value of the stock is higher than the exercise price.

- **Under water.** Options are *under water* (or *out of the money*) if the spread is negative; in other words, if the strike price is higher than the current value of the stock. There is no special tax significance to an option being under water, but the practical significance is that the option will not become valuable until the stock price recovers.

- **Option agreement.** When a company grants an option, it should provide you with an *option agreement*. This document spells out the key terms of your option, including the number of shares you can buy, the purchase price, and the time periods during which you're permitted to exercise the option.

- **Stock option plan.** Options are usually (but not always) issued pursuant to a formal *stock option plan* adopted by the board of directors and approved by the shareholders. The stock option plan often provides additional details concerning the terms of your options. Don't confuse the stock option plan with a prospectus or other summary. You need a copy of the plan itself to know precisely what your rights are.

- **Prospectus.** An option is an opportunity to invest, so it's appropriate for the company to provide a *prospectus* when granting options. This is a summary of the terms of the option and other information intended to help you decide whether to exercise the option.

It's *very important* to keep good records concerning equity compensation in general and stock options in particular. You should have a safe place where you keep your option agreement and a copy of the stock option plan. Keep any prospectus or other information materials, too. In a pinch, all of these documents may be useful in determining your rights.

More on Option Vesting

The words *vesting* and *vested* cause plenty of confusion. Partly this is because they're used differently depending on whether we're talking about *stock* or *stock options*. We say *stock* is vested at the point in time when you can quit your job and still keep the stock (or at least receive full value for it). Part VIII of this book deals with various rules for vesting of stock.

We mean something different when we say an *option* is vested. An option becomes vested at the point in time when you can exercise it (use it to buy stock). You don't necessarily get to keep an option when you quit your job, even if the option is vested. Most options terminate when your employment terminates or shortly thereafter, perhaps with some added leeway if your employment ends due to death or disability.

Your option may be vested even though the stock you buy under the option is *not* vested. If your company has an "early exercise" stock option plan (see Chapter 30), you may be in a position where you can exercise the option but you don't get to keep the stock if your employment terminates before a specified date.

The vesting rules for your stock option may appear in the option agreement or in the stock option plan. One of the first things you should do when you receive a stock option is determine when it becomes exercisable—in other words, when it vests. Many options vest gradually over a number of years.

> **Example:** You receive an option with a ten-year term, permitting you to buy 120 shares of your company's stock at a specified price. The option has a four-year vesting schedule. For the first year you can't exercise any of the option. Beginning on the first anniversary of the grant date, you can exercise 25% of the option. In other words, you can buy up to 30 shares. When you reach the second anniversary of the grant date, you can buy another 30 shares. Vesting is cumulative, so if you didn't buy the first 30 shares yet, you're now eligible to buy 60 shares. After four years have gone by, you're eligible to buy all 120 shares. You can exercise the entire option then, or part of it, or wait until later.

Option Economics

Suppose you hold an option to buy 1,000 shares of XYZ stock at $15 per share. The stock is trading at $20. What is the value of your option?

Many people make the mistake of saying the option has a value of $5,000. True, that's what you would receive if you exercised the option and immediately sold the stock. But the option is surely worth more than that.

An option has two kinds of value. One is called *intrinsic value*, and that is what the $5,000 represents. The other part of the value of an option is called the *time value*.

Consider the situation where you hold an option with no intrinsic value. The strike price is $20, and that's the current trading price, too. Is that option worthless, just because the spread is zero?

Certainly not. The option gives you an opportunity to obtain a bargain any time in the future if the stock's price goes up. Meanwhile, you aren't at risk of losing anything if the stock's price goes down. An option gives you the opportunity to profit from the upside without risking loss on the downside. That's a beautiful thing! It's the reason an option has value even if the spread is zero.

A complicated mathematical formula, called the *Black-Scholes formula*, is used to determine the value of stock options. Among other variables, the formula takes into account prevailing interest rates, the term of the option, the current price of the stock, and the stock's *volatility* (a measure of how much the price of this particular stock tends to zigzag up and down).

Chapter 12
Receiving Stock Options

Most nonqualified options, and *all* incentive stock options, are granted pursuant to a *stock option plan* that was adopted by the company's board of directors and approved by the shareholders. The board of directors, or a committee appointed by the board (usually called the *compensation committee*), may decide who receives the awards and the specific terms of the options. In some cases options are granted according to a formula set forth in the plan or in an employment agreement.

What You'll Receive

When a company grants an option it should provide certain documents. You should receive an *option agreement*, setting forth the specific terms of your option. If the option is issued under a plan, you should also receive a copy of the plan, which provides some general rules that govern all options. In many cases the company also provides a summary of the plan.

Make sure you keep these documents in a safe place. You should review them from time to time for planning purposes. At a minimum, you want to think about your options before the end of each year to determine whether to exercise some or all of the options by December 31 as part of your tax planning.

> **Note:** Many companies, including some large corporations, are lax when it comes to option documents. You may be asked to sign an option agreement that says you've received a copy of the plan, even though you've never seen the plan. Insist on receiving a copy of all relevant documents.

Typical Terms

Companies have great flexibility in the terms they can offer for options. Your options may differ from the typical option in a number of important ways. Yet it may be helpful to compare your option with the norm:

- The exercise price is usually set at (or near) the value of the stock at the time the option is granted. For incentive stock options, the price *must* be greater than or equal to the fair market value of the stock when the option is granted.

- The option becomes exercisable over a period of several years. For example, you may be able to exercise 25% after one year, 50% after two years, and so on. This is not a requirement, and some options are fully exercisable when issued.

- Cash payment is usually required at the time of exercise, but some companies make a form of "cashless exercise" available, and others will loan the money needed to exercise the option or arrange for such a loan from a broker or perhaps some other lender.

- The option expires ten years after it was issued, or earlier if employment terminates. You may or may not have a grace period (usually no more than three months) to exercise options at the time employment terminates. The grace period generally applies only to options that were exercisable when your employment terminated. Options that were scheduled to become exercisable on some later date typically expire when your employment ends, even if the date they would have become exercisable falls within the grace period.

Tax Consequences of Receiving an Option

With rare exceptions, there's no tax to pay, and nothing to report, at the time you receive a nonqualified option. The exceptions:

- You receive an option that's actively traded on an established securities market, or virtually identical to options that are actively traded. In many years of experience with options, I've never seen this rule apply.

- You receive a nonqualified option that's "in the money" to such a great extent at the time you receive it that the option is considered equivalent to owning the stock. For example, at a time when the stock is worth $40 per share you receive an option that permits you to buy the stock for $2 per share. This rule wouldn't apply to a nonqualified option that's only slightly in the money—for example, a nonqualified option with an exercise price of $35 that's issued when the stock value is $40. (ISOs *can't* be in the money when issued.)

In all other cases you have nothing to report at the time you receive an option. This is true even if the option is fully vested when you receive it.

No Section 83b Election

There's persistent confusion among taxpayers—and even among some tax professionals—about the section 83b election. This election can provide tax savings when you receive *stock* that's not vested. But the election doesn't apply when you receive an *option* except in the unusual situation where it's a publicly traded option. You may hear that there's an election you can make to reduce your tax when you receive a nonqualified option, but that's a mistake. The section 83b election is for stock only.

No Tax When Option Becomes Exercisable

You may receive an option that isn't immediately exercisable. You're permitted to exercise the option only if you continue to work for the company for a stated period.

> **Example:** You receive an option to buy 300 shares of the company's stock, but you're not permitted to exercise the option immediately. If you're still employed with that company a year later you become eligible to exercise half of this option. After another year of employment the option is fully exercisable.

The dates on which the option becomes exercisable are obviously significant, but you don't report income on these dates. The tax law takes no notice of them.

Tax Planning Starts Now

Tax planning for your options should begin the day you receive them. Begin by understanding your rights under the agreement and the stock option plan. Read these documents carefully, and make sure you can answer these questions:

- What is the earliest date you can exercise the option? Does it become exercisable in stages?

- What do you need to do when you exercise the option? Can you borrow to exercise the option? Can you pay the exercise price using stock you already own?

- What restrictions will be imposed on the stock you receive when you exercise the option? Can you sell it right away if you want to? Transfer it to a trust or family partnership? Does the company have the right to get the stock back under any circumstances?

- When will the option terminate? Can you exercise after your employment terminates? What if you die while holding the option?

Start thinking *now* about how and when you'll exercise the options. Will you exercise them all at once, or in stages over a number of years? What scenario will provide the best result for you? How will you come up with the money to exercise the options? And the money to pay the taxes? How will you handle an unexpected situation, such as loss of your job?

Chapter 13
Nonqualified Options and ISOs

Options you receive as compensation for services come in two flavors: *nonqualified options* and *incentive stock options*. If you're an employee, you may receive either type of option, or some of each. If you're not an employee, you can only receive nonqualified options. An option granted to a non-employee, such as an independent director or consultant, can't be an ISO.

Differences in Tax Treatment

Employees generally prefer incentive stock options. The special tax rules for ISOs are favorable to the holders of these options:

- You have to report income when you exercise a nonqualified option, but not when you exercise an incentive stock option.

- The income you report when you exercise a nonqualified option is compensation income. If you satisfy a special holding period requirement after exercising an incentive stock option, all your profit from the ISO will be long-term capital gain. You won't have to report any compensation income.

But ISOs bring bad news, too. When you exercise an incentive stock option, you're likely to have to pay alternative minimum tax (AMT). This tax may take away much of the benefit of not having to report income when you exercise your option. Apart from the cost of paying the tax, the complexity of dealing with the AMT can be daunting.

ISOs may be unattractive to employers for other reasons. Options don't qualify as incentive stock options unless they meet a list of requirements set forth in the Internal Revenue Code. Employers have more flexibility in dealing with nonqualified options. What's more, employers receive less favorable tax treatment for ISOs than for nonqualified options. The tax detriment to the company from choosing incentive stock options instead of nonqualified options may be greater than the tax benefit to the employee.

Which Do You Have?

Sometimes option holders are uncertain as to which type of option they have. This is the first thing you need to know! If you're unclear on this, here's how to find out.

Non-employees. If you're not an employee—in other words, you're not someone who has withholding taken from each paycheck and receives a W-2 at the end of the year—your option *has* to be a nonqualified option. The tax law doesn't permit companies to issue incentive stock options to non-employees. Even if your option says it's an ISO, it's a nonqualified option if you aren't an employee.

The option agreement. If you're an employee and unsure which type of option you have, the most reliable way to find the answer is to read the option agreement. You should have a copy of this document in your permanent records. If you don't, be sure to obtain a copy from the company.

- If the option agreement says the option is not an ISO, then that's your answer. Even if an option meets all other requirements to be an incentive stock option, the tax law says it's not an ISO if the option agreement declares that the option isn't an incentive stock option.

- If the option agreement says the option is an incentive stock option, then that *should* be your answer. Just saying that an option is an ISO isn't enough to make it one, however. The option has to satisfy a list of requirements in the tax law. For example, ISOs must be issued pursuant to a plan that has been approved by the company's shareholders. An incentive stock option can't be issued for a price that's lower than the fair market value of the stock on the date the option is granted, and can't extend for a period of more than 10 years. There are additional requirements, including special restrictions for individuals who own more than 10% of the stock of the company issuing the options.

Other rules. There are other rules that can change an incentive stock option to a nonqualified option. One is a $100,000 per year limit on the amount of incentive stock options you can receive. The limit applies to the year the option becomes *exercisable*, not the year you receive the option. But the limit is based on the value of the stock at the time the option is granted.

Example: You receive an incentive stock option that permits you to buy up to $400,000 worth of the company's stock. You can exercise one-fourth of the option immediately, but have to wait a year before exercising the second one-fourth, another year for the third one-fourth and one more year for the final one-fourth. This arrangement complies with the $100,000 limit, even if the stock is worth millions by the time you're eligible to exercise the last one-fourth.

The option described in the example consumes your entire limit for a four-year period. If you received any other options that became exercisable during that period, they would have to be nonqualified options.

Sometimes a company will issue options that exceed the limit without specifying that part of the option is a nonqualified option. That means you could have an option that *says* it's an ISO when in reality it's partly or entirely a nonqualified option. It's important to know how much of your option is nonqualified in this situation, because this will have great influence on your tax planning.

Termination of employment. The tax law says an option isn't an ISO if you're permitted to exercise it for more than a limited period after your employment terminates: one year if employment terminates because of disability, otherwise three months. Your option, or the plan under which it's issued, may provide a *shorter* period. If your ISO remains exercisable for a *longer* period, its status as an ISO will terminate.

Changing the agreement. Sometimes companies and option holders agree to change the terms of the options after they've been granted. If the option is an ISO, these changes have to be carefully reviewed. Some types of changes will be treated as a cancellation of the old option and issuance of a new one. The "new" option won't qualify as an incentive stock option if it doesn't meet all applicable requirements. In particular, it would be necessary to increase the exercise price if the value of the stock went up after the original issue date of the option. Great care is necessary whenever changing the terms of an incentive stock option that's already been issued.

Chapter 14
How to Exercise a Stock Option

In the rest of this book we'll talk about *when* to exercise options, and what your tax consequences will be. Before that knowledge can do you any good, you need to know *how* to exercise a stock option.

Step 1: Know your rights. To start with, you need to know whether you can exercise any of your stock options, and if so, which ones. Read your option agreement and relevant parts of the stock option plan. If you don't have copies of these documents, you should obtain them from the company.

You may find that you can exercise some of your stock options but not others. As indicated above, you may be able to exercise only *part* of a stock option. Even if your stock options are fully exercisable, you may wish to exercise only part of an option. Most plans permit partial exercise, subject to a minimum amount.

> **Example:** A typical provision might say you can exercise part of an option, but no fewer than ten shares at a time unless that's all you have at the time you exercise.

Step 2: Select a stock option. You may find that you have more than one stock option that's available for exercise. Unless you're planning to exercise all your options at once, you need to choose which stock option to exercise.

> **Example:** You hold an option to buy 100 shares at $18 per share, and another option to buy 200 shares at $15 per share. Both stock options are

fully exercisable. You want to exercise for 100 shares.

The easy thing to do is to exercise the option for 100 shares at $18. But if your plan permits, you can exercise half of the other option instead. That would cost $300 less because of the lower exercise price, but cause you to report an additional $300 of income.

At one time, the tax rules said you had to exercise incentive stock options in the same order you received them. Under this *sequential exercise rule,* if you hadn't exercised your oldest ISO, you couldn't exercise any other ISO. This rule is long gone. Unless your company has an outdated plan, you can exercise your options in any order.

Step 3: Select a method of payment. In the bad old days there was only one way to pay for stock when you exercised an option. In legal mumbo-jumbo, you had to *tender readily available funds.* In other words, you had to come up with cash.

That's still a popular method of payment, but some companies now make other alternatives available. The company may have an arrangement with a stock broker under which some or all of the stock is sold immediately to cover the exercise price and any tax withholding. See below for a discussion of *cashless exercise.*

Another possibility is to use stock you already own to pay the exercise price. For example, if it will cost $2,000 to exercise your option, you can turn in $2,000 worth of stock instead of $2,000 in cash. Not all companies offer this alternative. You may achieve benefits with this form of exercise that aren't available when you pay cash. Due to the complexity involved, Part VI of this book devotes several chapters to this form of exercise.

Step 4: Withholding. If you're an employee and you exercise a nonqualified option, the company has to withhold on the income you receive from exercising the option (see Chapter 41). Usually that means you have to come up with additional cash besides the option price.

Before you exercise your option, you should determine what your withholding obligation will be and how you'll meet it. The precise dollar amount won't be determined until you exercise the option, because the amount of income (and therefore the amount of withholding) is based on the value of the stock on the day you exercise.

Step 5: Exercise the option. Now you know exactly what you want to do and you're ready to exercise the option. Once again you have to look at the option agreement and the stock option plan to learn how to proceed. Most larger companies have a form you must fill out when you exercise an option. Other companies simply require notification in writing. In that case you would write a brief letter or memo something like this:

> *In accordance with my option agreement dated September 10, 1998 I hereby exercise my option to purchase 120 shares of common stock at the price of $30 per share. My check in the amount of $3,600 is attached.*

Chances are you won't be the first person to exercise an option at your company. If you have any doubt as to how to proceed, contact the appropriate office for instructions on how to proceed.

Cashless Exercise

Some employers make it easier for option holders to exercise their options by providing a way to combine the exercise of the option with a sale of some or all of the stock. In this situation you don't have to come up with any money to exercise the option or pay any withholding. That's why we call this a *cashless exercise* of your option.

Usually the company makes arrangements with a brokerage firm, which loans the money needed to buy the stock. The brokerage firm sells some or all of the stock immediately, with part of the proceeds being used to repay the loan—often the same day the loan was made. Another part of the sale proceeds will be used to cover any withholding requirement that applies, and any brokerage commissions and other fees. You receive whatever is left in the form of cash or unsold shares.

Not all companies permit this method of exercise. Some companies want to encourage option holders to retain the stock so they'll have an ongoing stake in the business. Others may be concerned that sales executed in this manner will depress the price of their stock. Review your option documents, or check with the company, to see if this method of exercising your options is available.

Tax consequences. The tax consequences of a cashless exercise are the same as if you took two separate steps: exercising the option, then selling the stock. The fact that you did both at once has no particular significance. Your sale will be short-term, of course. In the case of an incentive stock option, you'll have an early (disqualifying) disposition.

Frequently asked questions. Most confusion in this area comes when people don't realize that the single act of choosing a cashless exercise has to be reported as two transactions.

Q: My gain from exercising the option appears on my Form W-2 as wages—but Form 1099-B reports the full amount of proceeds, including the gain. Why is the same amount reported twice?

A: The same amount is *reported* twice, but it isn't *taxed* twice. Form 1099-B shows how much you received for selling the stock. When you figure your gain or loss, the amount reported on your W-2 is treated as an additional amount paid for the stock. (In other words, it increases your *basis*.) The effect is to reduce your gain or increase your loss, so you're not double taxed.

Q: Why do I have gain or loss when the stock was sold at the same time I exercised?

A: Often there's a gain or loss to report, for two reasons. First, the amount reported on your

W-2 as income is usually based on the stock's average price for the day you exercised your option, but the broker may have sold at a price slightly (or more than slightly) above or below that average price. And second, your sale proceeds are likely to be reduced by a brokerage commission and other costs, which can produce a small loss.

Can My IRA Exercise My Option?

You pay taxes, your IRA doesn't. That simple fact may lead you to the idea of having your IRA exercise your options. If it worked, you would get the benefit of the economic bargain inherent in your options, while the tax consequences would be deferred until you draw money from your IRA.

Unfortunately, options and IRAs don't mix. Regardless of whether you have nonqualified options or ISOs, you can't use your IRA to exercise options you received as compensation. This planning idea violates IRA rules and provides no tax benefits. Even if your company permits you to do this, and you slip it by your IRA provider, you won't be happy with the results.

To see what the problem is, ask yourself who exercised the option. There are only two candidates: you, or the IRA. Either answer has bad consequences.

You exercised. If you exercised the option (rather than the IRA), then you failed to shift the tax consequences of exercising from yourself to the IRA. You have to report income equal to the bargain element if you exercised a nonqualified option. The same is true if you exercised an incentive stock option, because your exercise is followed immediately by a disqualifying disposition of the stock. So you didn't accomplish anything positive.

At the same time you have a big negative. You aren't permitted to transfer property other than cash to an IRA, except in connection with a rollover from a qualified retirement plan or another IRA. Option plans are *not* qualified retirement plans. Violating this rule can result in severe penalties. End result: without accomplishing anything positive, you've created an expensive mess by violating the rule against contributing property to an IRA.

Your IRA exercised. But what if your IRA itself exercises the option? The answer is just as bad. The only way the IRA can exercise the option is if you have transferred the option from yourself to the IRA. Without such a transfer, it's you exercising the option, not the IRA. As we've seen, you're not permitted to transfer property other than cash to an IRA. Your option is property, so you've violated that rule if the IRA exercises the option.

You've also failed to shift the tax consequences. By definition, your option is a nonqualified option at this point, because ISOs are not transferable. The IRS has ruled that if a nonqualified option is transferred to another person, a subsequent exercise of the option results in compensation income to the original owner. Even if you could somehow get around the rule against transferring property to an IRA, you haven't avoided the need to report income upon exercise of the option.

In short. If this idea occurred to you as a way to handle your options, give yourself credit for creativity—and then move on to other ideas. Any way you look at it, this idea is a loser.

Part IV
Nonqualified Stock Options

Nonqualified stock options are the single most popular form of equity compensation. Companies like them because they provide a flexible and efficient way to attract, retain and motivate employees (and other service providers, such as directors and consultants). Workers like them because they represent an opportunity to grow wealth, with tax consequences deferred until the year of exercise.

This part of the book assumes you're familiar with the material in Part III.

Part IV
Nonqualified Stock Options

Chapter 15
Exercising Nonqualified Stock Options

Your nonqualified stock option gives you the right to buy stock at a specified price. You exercise that right when you notify the company of your purchase in accordance with the terms of the option agreement. The tax consequences of exercising a nonqualified stock option depend on whether the stock is vested when you receive it and the manner of exercising the option.

Normal Exercise

The normal way to exercise a nonqualified stock option is to pay the purchase price in cash. When you do this, your tax consequences are the same as for a non-option purchase of stock from your company. For a detailed discussion, turn to Chapter 9. Briefly, there are three possible treatments:

Stock is vested. You receive the stock with no strings attached (or the strings aren't enough to keep the stock from being vested). This is the most common situation. When this happens you report compensation income equal to the *bargain element* in your option: the difference between the fair market value of the stock on the day you exercised the option and the amount you paid for the stock. You have to report this income regardless of whether you sell the stock. If you're an employee, the company has to withhold income tax on this amount, and that usually means you have to come up with cash for the withholding in addition to the purchase price.

Example: Your option permits you to buy 1,000 shares at $25 per share. When you exercise, the stock is trading at $32. You'll report $7,000 of income (1,000 shares times the $7 spread per share). To exercise, you had to pay the $25,000 exercise price plus about $2,200 to cover withholding on the $7,000 of income.

Stock is not vested. Some companies require you to earn the right to keep the stock after you exercise the option. If there's a period of time when you can't keep the stock—or at least get full value for it—if you stop working for the company, your stock isn't vested. In this case, unless you file the *section 83b election* (see below), you report no income when you exercise the option. Instead, you report income when the stock vests. The amount of income is the difference between the fair market value of the stock *on the vesting date* and the amount you paid for it.

Example: Same as the previous example, except this time the option agreement says you have to sell the stock back at the $25 purchase price if your employment ends within the next year. You don't file the section 83b election. That means you don't report income when you exercise the option. A year later, when the stock vests, the value is $38 per share. At that time you report $13,000 of compensation income (1,000 shares times the difference between the $38 value and your purchase price of $25). Your company may require you to make a payment to cover withholding before releasing the shares to you.

Section 83b election. If your stock isn't vested when you receive it, you can choose to treat it as if it were vested. You do this by filing a "section 83b election" *within 30 days after you exercise the option*. If you file this election, you avoid having to report a larger amount of compensation income if the value of the stock goes up during the vesting period. Your tax treatment will be the same as in the first example above.

These rules are spelled out in more detail in Chapter 9.

Basis and Holding Period

It's important to keep track of your basis in stock. Basis determines how much gain or loss you report when you sell the stock. When you exercise a nonqualified option your basis is equal to the amount you paid for the stock *plus* the amount of income you report for exercising the option.

> **Example:** You bought stock worth $40 per share for $15 per share, reporting $25 per share of compensation income. Your basis is $40 per share: the $15 per share you paid to exercise the option plus the $25 per share you reported as compensation income. If you sell the stock later for $45 per share, your gain will be only $5 per share, even though you paid just $15 per share for the stock. The $5 per share profit will be capital gain, not compensation income.

For certain limited purposes (particularly under Section 16b of the Securities Exchange Act of 1934) you're treated as if you owned the stock during the period you held the option. This rule doesn't apply when you're determining what category of gain or loss you have when you sell the stock, though. You have to start from the date you bought the stock by exercising the option, and hold for more than a year to get long-term capital gain.

Cashless Exercise

Some companies make it easy for you to sell some or all of your stock at the same time you exercise the option. The sale proceeds cover your exercise price and withholding obligation, so this is sometimes called a *cashless exercise*. It may seem as if you had just a single transaction because everything happened at once, but when you exercise your options this way you have to report *two* transactions: exercise of the option (as described in this chapter) and sale of the stock (as described in the following chapter). See Chapter 14 for more discussion of cashless exercise.

Using Stock to Exercise an Option

Another way to exercise an option is to use stock you already own to pay the purchase price. Not all companies permit this method of exercise, however. The special tax considerations for this method of exercising options are explained in Part VI of this book.

Chapter 16
Selling NQO Stock

The tax rules for selling stock you receive from exercising a nonqualified stock option are relatively simple. With this type of option, you reported compensation income at the time of exercise or when the stock vested, so a sale produces capital gain or loss. You merely have to determine your holding period and basis, then report the sale as explained in Chapter 46.

Holding period. Your holding period for tax purposes begins when you exercise the option. You can't include the time you held the option. To get a long-term capital gain, you have to hold the stock at least a year and a day. If you sell earlier than that, any gain or loss will be short-term.

Basis. This is where you have to pay attention. Stock you buy through a broker has a basis equal to the amount you paid to acquire it (including brokerage commissions). Stock you buy when you exercise a nonqualified stock option has a basis equal to the amount you paid *plus the amount of income you reported when you exercised the option.*

Example: You exercised an option to buy stock for $20 per share when the stock was worth $35 per share. You reported compensation income equal to $15 per share. Two years later, you sold the stock at $45 per share.

When you report this sale on your tax return, you show a cost basis of $35 per share: the $20 per share you paid, plus the $15 per share of compensation income you reported. *If you forget to include the compensation income in your basis, you'll pay tax on that amount twice.*

Cashless Exercise

Some companies provide arrangements under which you can exercise your option and sell some or all of the stock at the same time. That way you don't have to come up with any cash at the time you exercise the option. This kind of *cashless exercise* is treated the same as two separate transactions: exercise of the option, followed by sale of the stock. For more on this subject see Chapter 14.

Stock Used to Exercise Option

Some companies permit you to use stock you already own to pay the purchase price when you exercise an option. Part VI of this book explains the special rules that apply in this situation.

Chapter 17
Gifts of Nonqualified Options

Many nonqualified stock option plans do not permit transfers of any kind. In recent years, some companies have made their nonqualified options transferable to a limited extent, usually only for estate planning purposes. You may be able to transfer your shares to family members, trusts, or a family partnership.

> The terms of your stock option agreement, or the stock option plan under which it was issued, determine whether the option is transferable.

No Income Shift

Such a transfer doesn't shift the income tax consequences of exercising the option. Even though you'll no longer own the option, you'll have to report income when the option is exercised, just as if you were the one to exercise it. The ability to transfer your option is not an opportunity for income tax planning.

Gift and Estate Tax

The benefit from transferring an option comes in connection with gift and estate tax. The option may be an asset that's likely to grow in value very quickly. That's precisely the kind of asset you want to get out of your estate if you're concerned about estate taxes. If you can move the option to an appropriate person or entity before it becomes extremely valuable you may save yourself some estate planning headaches later.

The IRS is aware of this opportunity. They haven't said there's anything wrong with doing this, but they laid out some ground rules in a pair of 1998 rulings that make it more difficult to shift valuable options without claiming much value.

Timing rule. You may receive a nonqualified option that doesn't permit immediate exercise. For example, the option may permit you to buy 300 shares at a specified price, but provide that you have to continue to work for the company one year to exercise the first 100, another year for the next 100 and yet another year before you can exercise the entire option.

The IRS has ruled that in this circumstance, you have not made a completed gift of the option until it becomes exercisable. The reasoning is that the option doesn't have any value unless you continue to work for the company. It isn't until you complete this service requirement that we can definitely say you transferred something of value.

This ruling is *bad news* for those who want to make an early transfer of nonqualified stock options. If you value the gift at the time of the transfer, it might be possible to argue that a discount applies because the donor has to keep working. By delaying the effective date of the gift, the IRS eliminates this possible discount. What's more important, if the company's stock rises in value during the period it takes for the option to become exercisable, the value of the option—and the potential gift tax liability—can increase dramatically. Depending on circumstances, a small percentage increase in the value of the stock can cause a large percentage increase in the value of the option.

If you're considering a gift of a nonqualified stock option, you should carefully consider the effect of this ruling. The ruling does not prohibit gifts prior to vesting, but such gifts become something of a gamble if an increase in the stock price can be anticipated. You don't know how large the gift is—and therefore the size of the gift tax implications—until after you've made the gift. To avoid unpredictable results, it may be prudent to wait until the options have vested before making a gift.

If the option vests in stages, the ruling states that the gift occurs in stages. It may be possible to handle this by giving only the vested portion of an option and retaining the part that isn't vested. The terms of the option agreement or the plan under which it was issued should tell you whether such a partial transfer is permitted.

Determining value. A companion ruling to the one described above provides a "safe harbor" for valuing certain compensatory stock options for gift tax purposes. This procedure applies only to options with respect to stock of public companies that are subject to FAS 123, an accounting rule that requires disclosure of certain information concerning compensatory options. The revenue procedure calls for the use of certain factors and methodologies used in FAS 123 reporting.

This procedure isn't mandatory. If you use a different valuation methodology you aren't necessarily wrong. But if you use the methodology in the ruling, you can be assured the IRS won't challenge it.

The ruling doesn't provide actual formulas for valuation. It calls for the use of standard valuation methods such as the Black-Scholes model, but the model must be adapted to the terms of the option and take into account anticipated dividends. In short, this is not a do-it-yourself procedure. But if you work for a company that's already hiring experts to value its options to comply with FAS 123, it's possible the same experts will provide the service of valuing options for gift tax purposes in accordance with the IRS rules.

Not Available for ISOs

You can't transfer an incentive stock option other than at death. This is a specific requirement of the Internal Revenue Code. If your option is transferable, it isn't an incentive stock option.

Don't Do This at Home

Estate planning is a very technical area. I have twenty years of experience as a lawyer, and I wouldn't dream of doing my own estate planning without consulting an expert. Lawyers aren't cheap, but the cost of estate planning expertise is a bargain compared to the cost of making a mistake in this area. That's especially true if you're dealing with complicated assets like equity compensation. When it comes to estate planning, get the kind of help that's appropriate to your level of wealth.

Chapter 18
Planning for Nonqualified Options

The most important planning concerns for nonqualified options can be summed up in seven words: When and how do you exercise them? There are no pat answers, or even reliable rules of thumb. You have to look at all aspects of the question and decide which are most important.

Compensation vs. Capital Gain

One of the most important factors in timing your exercise of nonqualified options is the difference between compensation income and capital gain. You'll have to report any growth in the value of the stock that occurs before you exercise the option as compensation income. Any increase in value that occurs after you exercise the option is capital gain. If you hold the stock more than a year after exercising the option, you'll report long-term capital gain, which is taxed at very favorable rates.

This consideration provides an argument for exercising your options early if the value of the company's stock is rising rapidly. Of course you won't benefit from this approach unless you hold the stock long enough to receive long-term capital gain treatment. And there's also the possibility that the anticipated growth in the value of the stock won't materialize.

If you exercise early, you're giving up part of the value of your option. When you think about it, the ability to pay the exercise price later is like receiving an interest-free loan. By exercising early, you're prepaying that loan. You're also giving up the chance to decide against exercise altogether if the company's fortunes decline. Still, in many cases it makes sense to consider early exercise to capture growth in value as long-term capital gain rather than compensation income.

Capital Loss Limitation

If you decide to hold the stock after exercising your nonqualified option, you should be aware of how the capital loss limitation will affect you if the value of the stock declines. You have to report compensation income when you exercise the option, but any loss on sale of the stock is a capital loss. Capital losses are allowed to the extent of capital gains plus $3,000 per year, with any excess carrying forward to the next year.

> **Example:** You exercise a nonqualified option, paying $30,000 to buy $100,000 worth of stock. You report $70,000 of compensation income. Later, you sell the stock for $60,000, reporting a loss of $40,000. Unless you have capital gains in the same year, you can claim only $3,000 of the loss. The remaining $37,000 carries forward.

The $3,000 capital loss limitation is a general rule. You would have the same consequences if you received a bonus and invested it in stock that subsequently declined in value. There's nothing unique about the way it applies when you exercise a nonqualified option. Yet it seems especially painful, and perhaps even unfair, when the $40,000 you lost—but can't deduct—is part of the $70,000 you reported as income when you exercised the option.

Diversification

Some people find that equity compensation represents a very high percentage of their net worth. Sound investment planning may call for you to diversify, so that your finances won't receive a crushing blow if the company falls on hard times. In some cases this investment consideration provides a strong reason to exercise options early, so that at least some of the stock can be sold and the proceeds invested more broadly.

Deferral

One of the most fundamental techniques of tax planning is *deferral*. Other things being equal, it's better to pay taxes later rather than sooner. Dollars that would otherwise be in the public treasury can be working for you in an investment account. Tax deferral is an argument for delaying the exercise of incentive stock options if they've already increased in value. The sooner you exercise, the sooner you'll have to report the income that's "built into" your options. This is a possible argument to *delay* exercise of your options.

Other things are never exactly equal, though. Deferral has to be a part of your thinking on when to exercise your options, but it isn't a controlling factor. In particular, as noted above, if the stock is going up in value, exercising sooner may mean paying *lower* taxes, even though it means paying taxes sooner.

Bunching of Income

If you have a large amount of income in one year, you're likely to find yourself in a higher tax bracket than usual. Besides the higher bracket, you may find yourself losing some tax benefits, such as personal exemptions and itemized deductions, because of rules that apply to higher-income taxpayers. The tax cost of taking a large chunk of income in a single year can be surprisingly high.

This consideration may provide an argument for exercising your options *gradually* over a number of years. Even if you're entitled to exercise the options all at once, it may make sense to divide them up. If this alternative is attractive, check your documents to see if partial exercise is permitted. Most option plans and option agreements allow you to exercise part of an option, subject to a minimum of some kind.

Method of Exercise

Some companies provide alternative methods of exercise, as described in Chapter 14. The availability of those alternatives may affect your planning for exercise of options.

For example, combined exercise of an option and sale of the stock eliminates the possibility of receiving long-term capital gain treatment for any portion of your profit.

If your company permits you to pay the option price with stock, this opportunity may influence your decision of when to exercise. You may want to exercise part of your option early to acquire stock you can use later to pay the purchase price when you exercise the rest of the option.

Part V
Incentive Stock Options

Incentive stock options (ISOs) are a form of equity compensation that provides unique tax benefits—and significant tax complexity. They aren't as widely used as nonqualified stock options, but their popularity is growing.

This part of the book assumes you're familiar with the option fundamentals explained in Part III.

Part V
Incentive Stock Options

Chapter 19
Overview of
Incentive Stock Options

Incentive stock options may appear to be very similar to nonqualified stock options. In fact, depending on the terms of your options, you may be able to lay a nonqualified option and an ISO side by side and see no difference at all, other than the fact that one is called an incentive stock option and the other is not. Yet ISOs are far more complex. Proper handling of them requires more knowledge, and more detailed planning, than are required for nonqualified options.

There's a reason to endure these headaches, though. Incentive stock options provide the possibility of paying significantly less tax than if you received nonqualifying options. If you can take full advantage of this opportunity, you'll benefit much more from an ISO than you would from a nonqualified option.

Alternative Minimum Tax

The biggest reason for the complexity of incentive stock options is the alternative minimum tax (AMT). This tax is so complicated that I devote a separate part of the book to explaining how it works. You can expect to pay AMT in the year you exercise an ISO unless you sell the ISO stock the same year. Some or all of the AMT may be allowed in a later year as a credit to reduce your regular income tax, however. You may find that you need professional help in forecasting the true cost of the AMT, and planning to minimize that cost.

Special Holding Period

Another source of complexity is the special holding period that applies to stock you acquire when you exercise an incentive stock option. Your tax consequences are different—and more favorable—if you hold the stock until the *later* of (a) one year after the date you exercised the option, or (b) two years after the date you received the option. Once you reach that point you can sell the stock without reporting any compensation income. All of your profit will be taxed at favorable capital gains rates. There are certain constraints on what you can do with the stock prior to satisfying this requirement. If you're considering disposing of the stock before that time period is up, you need to understand the consequences of an early disposition of ISO stock. Usually you'll have to report compensation income at that time.

Chapter 20
Exercising Incentive Stock Options

The most important difference between incentive stock options and nonqualified options is that you don't have to report compensation income when you exercise an ISO unless you sell the stock at the same time. If you hold your ISO stock long enough, you can avoid reporting compensation income altogether, so all your profit is taxed at favorable capital gain rates. But the tax law also taketh away. You may have to pay a significant amount of tax when you exercise your ISO because of the alternative minimum tax (AMT).

This chapter explains general rules that apply when you exercise incentive stock options. Be sure to consult the appropriate chapters in Part VI of this book if your option plan has special features:

- The opportunity to use stock you already own to pay the exercise price for your option.

- The opportunity for "early exercise," where you buy stock before it's vested.

Regular Tax Treatment

For purposes of the regular income tax, the exercise of an incentive stock option is a non-event. Unless you sell the stock at the same time, exercising the option doesn't affect the amount of regular income tax you report in any way.

> As explained in Chapter 15, you have to report compensation income when you exercise a nonqualified option.

Because you don't report any income when you exercise an incentive stock option, your basis for the stock you acquired is simply the amount you paid for it. Your holding period begins when you acquire the stock. You can't include the period for which you held the option.

Alternative Minimum Tax

So much for the good news. The bad news is that the exercise of an incentive stock option gives rise to an "adjustment" under the AMT. The adjustment is precisely the amount you would have reported as compensation income if you exercised a nonqualified option instead of an ISO. In other words, it's equal to the amount by which the fair market value of the stock exceeds the amount you paid for it—otherwise known as the *spread* or *bargain element.*

> The AMT adjustment only applies if you hold the ISO stock at the end of the calendar year in which you exercise the option. If you dispose of your ISO stock before then, you don't report an AMT adjustment. See Chapter 21.

The AMT adjustment has three consequences.

AMT liability. First and most obviously, you may have to pay AMT in the year you exercise an incentive stock option. There's no way to determine the amount of AMT you'll pay simply by looking at the amount of the bargain element when you exercise the option. This adjustment may be the event that triggers AMT liability, but the *amount* of liability depends on many other aspects of your individual income tax return. You may find that you can exercise some ISOs without paying any AMT at all. If your bargain element is large, though, you should expect to pay as much as 28% or more of the bargain element as AMT. The maximum rate for the AMT is 28%, and for large dollar amounts you can use that percentage as a reasonable guesstimate of your AMT liability. The tax resulting from a single item can be greater than that percentage, though, because of the way various features of the alternative minimum tax interact.

> AMT is included when you determine how much estimated tax you have to pay. See Chapter 42.

AMT credit. The second consequence from the AMT adjustment is that some or all of your AMT liability will be eligible for use as a credit in future years. This credit can only be used in years when you *don't* pay AMT. It reduces your regular tax, not your AMT. It's called the AMT credit because it's a credit for having paid AMT in the past.

In the best case, the AMT credit will eventually permit you to recover all of the AMT you paid in the year you exercised your incentive stock option. When that happens, the only effect of the AMT was to make you pay tax *sooner*, not to make you pay *more* tax than you would have paid. But for various reasons you can't count on being able to recover all of the AMT in later years, especially when large dollar amounts are involved.

AMT basis. The third consequence from the AMT adjustment is very important—and easy to overlook. We noted earlier that the stock you acquire when you exercise an ISO has a basis equal to the amount you paid. But the stock has a different basis for purposes of the alternative minimum tax. The stock's AMT basis is equal to the amount you paid *plus* the amount of the AMT adjustment. That means you'll report a smaller amount of gain for AMT purposes when you sell the stock.

> **Example:** You exercise an ISO, paying $35 per share when the value is $62 per share. You report an AMT adjustment of $27 per share. Later, after satisfying the holding period for ISO stock, you sell the stock for $80 per share. For purposes of the regular income tax you report gain of $45 per share ($80 minus $35). But for AMT purposes you report gain of only $18 per share. Your AMT basis

is equal to the $35 you paid plus the $27 adjustment you reported.

The difference in the amount of gain results in a *negative adjustment* for purposes of the AMT. This negative adjustment can be used to cancel out a positive adjustment you have from exercising more ISOs in the year you sell this stock, perhaps enabling you to exercise ISOs without incurring more AMT liability. If you don't exercise more options in the year you sell your ISO stock, the negative adjustment will help you use your AMT credit. For further explanation, see Part VII.

> If you overlook the higher AMT basis of your ISO stock when you sell it, you may end up unnecessarily paying double tax with respect to your ISO.

State Taxes

Some states (notably California, home of many companies that provide incentive stock options) have their own version of the alternative minimum tax. When you figure the cost of exercising your ISOs, don't forget the possibility of paying state AMT.

There's potential for a double whammy here. State income tax (including state AMT) is a deduction on your federal return if you itemize. But the deduction isn't allowed when you calculate your federal AMT. Paying state AMT can increase your federal AMT!

Chapter 21
Early Disposition of ISO Stock

Incentive stock options provide a unique benefit: the ability to avoid reporting any of your profit as compensation income. If you wait long enough before selling your stock, all your profit will be long-term capital gain. This chapter is about situations where you *don't* wait long enough.

> **Tax lingo:** If you sell or otherwise dispose of your ISO stock before the end of the special holding period described below, you've made a *disqualifying disposition*. We use the term *early disposition* to mean the same thing.

Special Holding Period

To avoid an early disposition you have to hold the stock you acquired by exercising your ISO beyond the *later* of the following two dates:

- One year after the date you exercised the ISO, or

- Two years after the date the company granted the ISO to you.

Many employers don't permit exercise of an ISO within the first year after the employee receives it. If that's the case you don't have to worry about holding more than two years after the date your employer granted the option. You'll automatically satisfy that test if you hold more than a year after the date you exercise the option. If you can exercise in the first year, though, and you choose to do so, you'll have to hold the stock more than a year to avoid an early disposition.

> **Example:** You receive an incentive stock option and exercise it six months later. If you sell the stock thirteen months after exercise, you'll have an early (or disqualifying) disposition even though you held the stock more than a year. The reason: your sale occurred less than two years after you received the option.

What Is a Disposition?

Everyone understands that a *sale* of ISO stock within the special holding period results in a disqualifying disposition. Other types of transfers may or may not be considered dispositions for this purpose.

Death of shareholder. A transfer that occurs as a result of your death is not a disposition for purposes of this rule. Your death during the special holding period will not trigger compensation income.

Transfer to spouse. A transfer of the stock to your spouse—or to a former spouse in connection with a divorce—is not a disqualifying disposition. Following such a transfer, the spouse receiving the stock is subject to the same rules as the one who transferred the stock. If you receive ISO shares from your spouse you should also obtain essential information for tax reporting:

- The date when the special holding period ends.

- The cost basis of the shares.

- The value of the shares on the date the option was exercised.

Gifts. Transfers at death and gifts to your spouse are covered by the rules described above. All other gifts are dispositions. You'll have to report compensation income if you give your ISO stock to an individual or to a charity before the end of the special holding period.

Trusts. A custodial account under the Uniform Transfers to Minors Act (or the Uniform Gifts to Minors Act) is *not* a trust. Transfers to such accounts are gifts, and count as dispositions.

A transfer of ISO stock to a *revocable* trust should not be treated as a disposition. You can terminate this kind of trust and take the stock and other property back whenever you want. For that reason, the tax law treats you as if you still own the stock after you transfer it to a revocable trust.

You've made a disposition, though, if you transfer the stock to an *irrevocable* trust. This type of trust doesn't let you take the stock back out. Generally you'll want to avoid making such a transfer during the special holding period, because it means having to report compensation income.

Transfer to broker. Transferring stock certificates to a broker who will hold the stock in street name isn't a disposition. Any transfer of the shares from the brokerage account will be treated as a transfer by you.

Short sales. The IRS takes the position that a short sale of your company's stock while you hold ISO stock is a disposition, even if the constructive sale rules don't apply.

Example: You exercised an ISO in March, buying 1,000 shares. In June, you sold short 1,000 shares, while continuing to hold your ISO shares. In September you closed the short sale by purchasing shares in the stock market. You never sold the ISO shares, and the constructive sale rules don't apply. Yet the IRS position is that you made a disqualifying disposition in June when you made the short sale.

Market options. Within limits, you can use options you buy in the stock market to protect your gains in ISO stock without causing a disqualifying disposition. For example, you may be able to buy a put option that protects you against a decline in the value of the stock. Some of the tax consequences of doing this are unclear, however. See Chapter 45 for more on this subject.

Borrowing. Using the stock as collateral for a loan is *not* a disposition. For example, you can hold the stock in a margin account with your broker without triggering compensation income. Of course, you'll have a disposition if the stock is sold to meet your margin requirements, or is otherwise seized as collateral. See below for bankruptcy, however.

Bankruptcy. A special rule protects you from having a disqualifying disposition in bankruptcy. You don't have a disposition when the stock is transferred to a bankruptcy trustee, or when the trustee transfers it to a creditor in satisfaction of a liability.

Regular Tax and Disqualifying Dispositions

The tax consequences of an early disposition apply in the year the disposition occurs. You aren't supposed to go back and amend the return for the year you exercised the option, if that was an earlier year.

Sale to an unrelated person. If your disqualifying disposition is a sale of shares to an unrelated person, your tax consequences are as follows:

- For a sale below the amount you paid for the shares, you don't report any compensation income. Your loss on this sale is reported as a capital loss.

- For a sale above the amount you paid for the shares but no higher than the value of the shares as of the date you exercised the option, report your gain on the sale as compensation income (not capital gain). You need to report the sale on Schedule D (used to report capital gains and losses), but your basis should be equal to the selling price, so that you have no gain or loss on the sale.

- If you sell your shares at a price that's higher than the value of the shares as of the date you exercised the option, you report two different items. The bargain element when you exercised the option (the difference between the value of the shares as of that date and the amount you paid) is reported as compensation income. Any additional gain is reported as capital gain (which may be long-term or short-term depending on how long you held the stock).

Other dispositions. If you had a disqualifying disposition from a transaction other than a sale to an unrelated person (such as a gift to someone other than your spouse, or a sale to a related person other than your spouse), it's possible that the rules for that type of transfer don't permit the deduction of losses. If your disqualifying disposition comes from a type of transaction where a deduction for losses is not permitted, the following rules apply:

- You have to report the full amount of the bargain element from when you exercised the option as compensation income. That's true even if the value of the stock has gone down since the date you exercised the ISO.

- If the transaction requires you to report gain (such as a sale to a related person other than your spouse), any gain that exceeds the amount of compensation income should be reported as capital gain (which may be long-term or short-term depending on how long you held the stock).

Compensation but no withholding. The IRS doesn't require withholding in connection with a disqualifying disposition of ISO stock. Many years ago the IRS announced that it was going to rethink that position, but it never issued new rules. Even though you may have compensation income under the rules described above, you shouldn't have to pay withholding or social security tax.

AMT Consequences

The alternative minimum tax consequences of an early disposition depend on whether it occurs in the same year you exercise your option.

Disposition in year of exercise. When your disposition occurs in the same year you exercised the option, you have nothing to report for AMT purposes. You don't report anything for exercising the option, and you don't report anything for disposing of the stock, because the two actions cancel each other out under the alternative minimum tax.

Disposition in a later year. When you make an early disposition, but not in the same year you exercised the option, your situation is a little more complicated. The AMT adjustment you reported in the year you exercised the option will give you a negative AMT adjustment (an adjustment in your favor) in the year of the disposition. That adjustment should make it easier for you to claim a credit for the AMT you paid in the year of exercise. See Part VII for more information.

Chapter 22
Sale of Mature ISO Stock

Once you satisfy the special holding period for stock acquired with an incentive stock option, you have *mature ISO stock*. A sale or other disposition of this stock isn't a disqualifying disposition. Any profit you have from a sale will be capital gain, *not* compensation income. In addition, selling this stock may help you claim an AMT credit and recover some or all of the alternative minimum tax you paid when you exercised the option.

Regular Tax Consequences

For purposes of the regular tax, selling mature ISO stock is just like selling stock you bought on the open market. Your basis is equal to the amount you paid for the stock, and your holding period began when you exercised the option. For more information on reporting sales of stock, see Chapter 46.

AMT Consequences

It's *extremely important* to understand, and properly report, the alternative minimum tax consequences of selling mature ISO stock. A mistake here can cost you a lot of money.

When you exercised you ISO you had to report an *AMT adjustment* that may have required you to pay alternative minimum tax. Regardless of whether the adjustment resulted in a need to pay AMT, the adjustment caused you to have a *dual basis* in your ISO stock. For purposes of the regular income tax your basis is simply the amount you paid to buy the stock. But when it comes to the AMT, you increase your basis by the amount of the AMT adjustment.

The upshot is that you'll report a *negative* AMT adjustment—an adjustment in your favor—when you sell your ISO stock. On the most recent version of Form 6251 (the form used to report your AMT calculation), the adjustment appears on line 9 and should be entered as a negative number. This adjustment can reduce your taxes.

- If you're otherwise subject to AMT liability in the year you sold the ISO stock (perhaps because you exercised a new ISO), the negative adjustment will reduce or eliminate the AMT you pay in the current year.

- If you aren't subject to AMT liability in the year you sold the ISO stock, the negative adjustment increases the gap between your regular tax and the tax that's calculated under the AMT rules. The result may be a larger *AMT credit* in the year you sell the ISO stock.

Part VII of this book provides more information on the alternative minimum tax. In particular, see Chapter 33 concerning dual basis and Chapter 34 for more about the AMT credit.

Chapter 23
Planning for Incentive Stock Options

Planning for incentive stock options is largely a matter of timing. You have two major issues:

- When should you exercise your options?

- Should you hold the stock long enough to satisfy the special holding period?

The bad news is that this is a *very* complicated area of tax planning. It isn't amenable to simple rules of thumb. Answers depend on the unique circumstances of each individual. Often there is relatively little that can be done to improve the tax results.

The good news? You may have a fair amount of control over the timing of your tax consequences if you plan far enough ahead.

When to Exercise

Unless you sell your stock at the same time you buy it (see *When to Sell*, below), your tax concerns when you exercise an ISO have to do with the alternative minimum tax. This tax is very complicated, and the way it applies to you depends very much on your individual circumstances.

> Part VII of this book is devoted to the alternative minimum tax. *Read it.* Even if you expect to consult a tax professional for planning advice on your ISOs, you need to understand generally how these rules work to make intelligent decisions.

Exercise over several years. The number of people affected by the AMT, even without exercising incentive stock options, increases every year. Congress made some foolish choices when they wrote this law back in 1986, and those choices are coming home to roost now. You can be hit with AMT liability simply because you have a large number of dependents!

Still, most people don't pay AMT in a normal year. For these people, there's usually a bit of leeway before the AMT will hit, even if they do something that normally gives rise to AMT. You may find that you can exercise at least some of your incentive stock options without incurring any AMT at all. Even if you'll be hit with some AMT, it may make sense for you to spread your exercise of ISOs over a number of years, to take maximum advantage of the amount of leeway you have in each of those years.

Spreading your exercise over a number of years can be helpful in other respects, too. You won't need to come up with such a large dollar amount all at once to exercise your options—and pay your taxes. You may be able to sell some of the stock from your earlier exercise of ISOs to pay the exercise price (and taxes) on a later exercise. You may even be able to use shares you bought earlier to pay for shares you buy later, if your company permits this form of exercise. What's more, the sale of earlier shares can create a favorable AMT adjustment that offsets the AMT adjustment on a subsequent exercise, reducing or eliminating AMT liability on the later purchase.

Critical time periods. There are two critical times to think about exercising options. One is before the end of the year. December 31 is your last chance to exercise an option in the current year. If you have an opportunity to save money by exercising this year, that opportunity will be gone when January rolls around.

It may be even more helpful if you can think about exercising *early* in the year—no later than early April. Exercising your option during this time period may enable you to satisfy the special holding period requirement and sell some or all of the stock by tax time without making a disqualifying disposition. This is one way to handle the problem of having a large AMT liability when you exercise your options.

> **Example:** Your options have increased in value by about $400,000. You anticipate having more than $100,000 of AMT liability in the year you exercise the options. You exercise in March, 2000, then hold the stock for a year and sell at least enough to pay the tax by April 15, 2001.

You don't have this opportunity if you exercise your options later in the year. To pay the tax by April 15, you would either have to come up with the $100,000 from some other source (perhaps borrowing against the stock), or sell some of the stock in a disqualifying disposition that would cause you to report compensation income.

Note that this approach only works if you've held the *option* for a year prior to exercise. The special holding period for ISO stock is satisfied on the *later* of the date that's one year after you exercised the option or two years after the option was granted. In the example above, if the option was granted in October, 1999, the sale of stock in April, 2001 would be a disqualifying disposition.

Capital loss limitation. There's another reason to exercise early in the year if you plan to hold the stock. Doing so gives you a chance to dodge a bullet if the value of your stock declines. A sale before the end of the year will avoid the AMT capital loss limitation.

This is a fairly obscure issue that most tax pros may overlook. The problem arises because sale of your ISO stock can produce a gain for regular tax purposes but a loss under the AMT. Your AMT loss, when combined with other gains and losses, is limited to $3,000. That can make it hard to use your AMT credit. The problem can arise even if you make a disqualifying disposition. But if you sell the stock in the same year you exercised the option, a special rule lets you escape the AMT capital loss limitation for those shares.

If you exercise your ISO in January, you have eleven months to see whether a decline in the stock's value will snare you in the AMT capital loss limitation. If the problem arises, you can consider selling some or all of the stock in December. For any shares you hold at the end of the year you'll have less than a month to wait until you can sell without a disqualifying disposition. Your risk of being trapped by the AMT loss limitation is small. By contrast, if you exercise ISOs in December, the chances are very good that any decline in value will occur too late for you to take action.

> **Example:** You exercise an ISO in January, when the spread is $200,000. You plan to hold the stock for a year before selling. In December, you find that the value of your shares has declined by $170,000. You still have a profit of $30,000.
>
> If you hold your shares until January, you'll pay over $50,000 in AMT for the year of exercise. You'll recover some of that as an AMT credit in the following year, but only a small amount because your favorable adjustment is only $33,000. That's the gain you have for purposes of the regular tax plus the $3,000 permitted under the AMT capital loss limitation. In this situation, you may be out of pocket more than $30,000 in taxes, even though your profit was only $30,000!
>
> Now look at what happens if you sell in December. The sale occurs in the same year you exercised the option, so you don't have an AMT adjustment. You've made a disqualifying disposition, so your $30,000 profit is compensation income, not capital gain. But your tax is only about $10,000, and that's a lot better than paying over $50,000 and getting a small fraction of that amount back the following year.

Buying the dip. There's one other timing issue that bears mention, even though it's a very difficult one to manage. The lower your company's trading value is when you exercise your option, the smaller your AMT consequences. If you can manage to buy at a time when the value is low—what traders call *buying the dip*—you'll reduce your AMT. The trouble is that the stock market is notoriously unpredictable. If you happen to have expertise in analyzing trading trends you may want to apply that knowledge in timing the exercise of your options. Unless you have a great deal of experience in this area, however, you should focus on other issues. Waiting around for the stock's price to dip could leave you sitting on the sidelines while the value rises, increasing your tax cost with each upward tick.

When to Sell

Some advisors suggest that the only correct way to handle incentive stock options is to plan on holding the stock until you satisfy the special holding period. Usually this is the choice that minimizes taxes, but it may not be the right choice for you. It isn't necessarily a bad move to sell some or all of your stock at the same time you exercise the option, or before the end of the year you exercised the option.

The most important point to have in mind is that the decision to sell or hold your ISO stock isn't purely a tax decision. It's also—in fact, *primarily*—an *investment* decision. There's no question you'll be better off holding the stock if its price climbs while you hold it. Similarly, no matter what your tax situation is, selling immediately is the better move if the stock is about to tank.

The tax consequences explained here merely shift the risk factors somewhat. If you gain a significant benefit from satisfying the special holding period for ISO stock, you have more profit potential from holding the stock, and less risk of loss, than an ordinary holder of your company's stock. That doesn't necessarily make it a wise investment for you, particularly if a very large percentage of your net worth is tied up in that stock. You need to consider the tax advantages of holding in light of your investment objectives and your view of your company's prospects during that period of time.

Best case scenario. In the best case scenario, you're able to exercise your incentive stock option without incurring any alternative minimum tax liability. This is possible for some people, but usually occurs only when the bargain element on exercise of the option is relatively small. In this situation you receive a double tax benefit from holding the stock versus selling:

- You postpone the tax by at least a year, and

- Your tax is at long-term capital gains rates rather than your ordinary tax rate.

The combination of these two factors can be very attractive. If you're in the 31% bracket, for example, your choice might be to pay $3,100 this year or $2,000 next year. There's no question which of these is better—from a tax perspective. But if the stock goes down more than $1,100, you could still come out behind by deciding to hold.

Second best case. The second best case, which is more likely than the first one, especially for a medium sized option exercise, is that you have to pay AMT in the year of exercise, but you're able to recover that amount in a later year because of the AMT credit. If you can recover the entire amount of AMT in a later year, the only effect of the AMT is to cause you to pay taxes *sooner.* You don't pay any *more* tax because of the AMT. So you lose some or all of the timing benefit mentioned above for the best case scenario, but you still gain the advantage of shifting income from your ordinary tax bracket into the tax rate for long-term capital gain. Buying and holding may still be very attractive in this situation, but you don't get quite as much bang for your buck as if you could avoid AMT altogether.

Worst case scenario. Unfortunately, some people will find that they can't recover the full cost of the AMT, even when they sell all their ISO stock. They may be left with an unused credit that they can use only in dribs and drabs over coming years, or some of the credit may have been swallowed up by a quirk in the way AMT applies to long-term capital gains (see Chapter 32). In this situation, alternative minimum tax is no longer just a timing issue. It's affecting the total amount of tax you have to pay in connection with your ISOs.

This problem is most likely to arise when dealing with large dollar amounts. A big reason for the problem is that AMT applies at rates up to 28%, while the long-term capital gains rate is only 20%.

> **Example:** You exercise an ISO when the spread is $1,000,000, and pay approximately $280,000 in AMT. When you sell the stock, your tax rate for the $1,000,000 of gain is 20%, so you use only about $200,000 of the AMT credit that year.

The remaining $80,000 of AMT credit would still be available for future use, and may provide a noticeable benefit for you in years to come. It's possible, though, that you'll never recover the entire credit. Even if you do, the delay in receiving the benefit greatly reduces its value.

It's worth repeating that this circumstance doesn't mean it's foolish to hold the stock. You may still receive some tax benefit from holding some or all of the stock. Even if there's no tax benefit at all, you can benefit if the stock's value climbs while you hold it. The point is to make your investment decision with the benefit of knowing the tax consequences. In this worst case scenario, the tax benefits of holding may be too small to significantly influence your choice between holding the stock or selling it.

Detailed analysis. Fully understanding your tax results from holding the stock requires a difficult, detailed analysis. The AMT is so complicated that its effects can surprise even a seasoned tax pro. You can't tell for certain what your tax consequences will be until you've done a full projection of your tax return for both the year of exercise and the year of sale.

I'm all in favor of such analysis, but only after you've thought about the investment issue. Do you really want to hold this much of your company's stock for that period of time? Will a shift in the tax consequences change your feeling about that?

State Income Tax

There are two important reasons to think about state income tax when you plan for the exercise of your incentive stock options. The first is that some states have their own alternative minimum tax. If you live in California, for example, you can expect to pay a hefty amount of state AMT on top of federal AMT when you exercise an incentive stock option.

You also need to think about state taxes as they affect your federal AMT. State taxes are deductible if you itemize, but the deduction isn't allowed for AMT purposes. Proper timing of the payment of state taxes can reduce the amount of AMT you pay, or increase the amount of AMT that qualifies for the AMT credit. You may not have a lot of control over when you pay your state income taxes, but to the extent you have such control you may save money if you time those payments for maximum advantage in connection with the federal AMT.

Part VI
Special Features for Options

Some companies allow you to pay the exercise price for an option by turning in shares of stock you already own. This opportunity isn't available under all stock option plans, so check first before you make plans. If your company allows you to do this, read the chapters in this part that apply to your situation.

Chapter 24 describes the process in general. Turn to Chapter 25 if you're thinking of using stock to exercise a nonqualified stock option. Chapter 26 deals with the tax consequences when you use stock to exercise an incentive stock option.

There are some interesting—and unclear—issues involving early disposition of ISO stock after you use stock to exercise an incentive stock option. Chapter 27 tells how you might profit from these rules—or how you might get burned. Another advanced topic appears in Chapter 28: how you may be able to defer income from exercising nonqualified stock options, if your company has the proper arrangements in place.

Finally, we cover two relatively recent innovations: reload options in Chapter 29, and "early exercise" stock option plans in Chapter 30.

Part VI
Special Features for Options

Chapter 24
Using Stock to Exercise Options

Some companies permit option holders to use shares of stock they already own to pay the purchase price when they exercise an option to buy new shares.

> **Example:** You have an option to buy 600 shares of stock for $5 per share. The current value of the stock is $12 per share. To exercise the option you can pay $3,000 in cash—or, if your company permits, you can "pay" $3,000 in stock. You would turn in 250 shares (250 times the current value of $12 equals $3,000) and receive 600 shares (an increase of 350 shares).

This form of exercise is often very convenient because it relieves the option holder of the need to come up with cash to exercise the option. (Cash will still be required to cover withholding and other tax liabilities, however.) The tax results may be favorable when compared to an alternative where you sell stock to come up with the cash to exercise your option.

Availability

Not all companies permit this form of exercise. The company may not like this approach because it puts fewer shares in the hands of option holders compared to a cash exercise. Possibly the company (or its share-holders) believe that a cash exercise shows greater commitment or has greater integrity. Whatever the reason, you can't *assume* this method of exercise is available. Read your option agreement and the stock option plan under which it was issued, and ask the appropriate person at your company if you're still unsure.

Of course this method of exercise isn't available if you don't own stock in the company. In that case you'll need to use cash, at least for your first purchase. After that you may be able to use stock you bought from an earlier exercise of an option to exercise later options. Be sure to understand the tax consequences before adopting this approach.

Certification Instead of Exchange

You might wonder whether it's necessary to have an actual exchange of shares. After all, the shares you receive in the exchange are identical to the shares you surrender. If you're going to turn in 250 shares to receive 600 that are exactly the same, why not just hold onto the 250 shares and receive 350 new shares?

In private letter rulings, the IRS has said you can do exactly that. The rulings describe a process in which you certify that you own the shares that are needed for the exchange. If the shares are held by a registered securities broker in street name on your behalf, you would submit a notarized statement attesting to the number of shares owned. If you hold the certificates yourself, you would submit the certificate numbers, which can be checked against the records of the transfer agent. The IRS says this is good enough to count as constructive delivery of the shares.

If available, this approach can save time and money in situations where it may be costly to actually tender the shares. If you're using the shares as collateral for a loan, for example, you may need the lender's permission to transfer the shares. In any event, the paperwork involved in the certification process is likely to be less cumbersome than tendering the shares.

Tax Consequences

The tax consequences of using stock to exercise an option depend on the type of option. See Chapter 25 for non-qualified options, and Chapters 26 and 27 for incentive stock options.

Chapter 25
Using Stock to Exercise
Nonqualified Options

Chapter 24 describes the general idea of using stock to exercise options. This chapter explains the tax consequences when you use stock to exercise a nonqualified option. These consequences are unusual and interesting. You're treated as if two separate things happened:

- You made a *tax-free exchange* of old shares for an equal number of new shares (the "exchange shares"), *and*

- You received *additional* shares (the "added shares") for zero payment.

As to the *exchange* shares you don't report any income. The shares you receive in the exchange have the same basis and holding period as the shares you turned in. It's as if you simply continued to hold the old shares.

As to the *added* shares, you have to report the value as compensation income when you receive them (or when they vest, if later), the same as if you received a grant or award of stock, as explained in Chapter 9. Those shares take a basis equal to the amount of compensation income you report, and your holding period begins when you acquire them (or when they vest).

Example: You have an option to buy 600 shares of stock for $5 per share (a total of $3,000). You exercise the option by turning in 250 shares worth $12 per share. Assuming the shares are vested when you receive them, you would end up with 250 shares that have the same basis and holding period as the shares you turned in, plus 350 shares with a basis of $12 per share and a holding period that begins when you acquire the shares.

Identification. When you decide to sell some of your shares, it will be important to determine which shares you want to sell. In some cases you'll want to sell the newer shares because they have a higher basis. In other cases you may want to sell the older shares to get long-term gain instead of short-term gain. Be sure you understand the principles and procedures for identifying shares as explained in Chapter 43.

Using ISO shares. It may be possible to use shares you own from a previous exercise of an incentive stock option to pay the purchase price on exercise of a nonqualified stock option. This exchange will not be treated as a disposition of the ISO stock, but the exchange shares will *continue* to be ISO shares. That means a subsequent sale of those shares may cause you to report compensation income if you haven't satisfied the special holding period. In the example above, if you turned in 250 ISO shares, then 250 of the shares you received in the exchange would be treated as ISO shares with the same basis and holding period as the shares you turned in.

> **Caution:** The same rule doesn't apply if you use ISO shares to exercise an ISO. Chapter 26 explains the rules for using stock to exercise an ISO.

Evaluation

This method of exercising an option doesn't produce any magical benefits. The greatest advantage is in situations where you would have to sell stock you already own in order to come up with the money you need to exercise the option. In this case, using stock to exercise the option permits you to avoid reporting gain from a sale of those shares. But you'll report the gain eventually, so this is a tax deferral, not a tax reduction.

If one of the alternatives available to you is combined exercise and sale (or *cashless exercise*), as explained in Chapter 15, you should find that the method described in this chapter has almost exactly the same consequences— provided that you sold only enough of the newly purchased shares to pay the exercise price. Normally, the sale portion of that transaction produces very little gain or loss, and you end up holding the same number of shares (and reporting the same amount of income) as if you had used stock to exercise your option.

Of course, you don't necessarily have to use either of these "cashless" methods to exercise your option. You can use funds you have available from another source— savings, perhaps, or taking out a loan—to exercise the option. Comparing this alternative to a "cashless" exercise is an investment question. Do you want to maximize your holding in the company's stock? If so, use cash from another source to exercise your option. If not, consider a cashless form of exercise, if the company makes it available.

Chapter 26
Using Stock to Exercise ISOs

Chapter 24 describes the general idea of using stock to exercise options. This chapter explains the tax consequences when you use stock to exercise an incentive stock option.

Tax Authorities

The tax consequences described below are based in large part on *proposed regulations* and *private letter rulings*. These authorities aren't binding on the IRS, so it's possible in theory that the IRS could challenge a return filed on the basis of these rules. As a practical matter that's very unlikely because the IRS position on these matters hasn't changed in many years.

Source of the Old Stock

The tax consequences of this form of exercise depend on whether or not you use *immature ISO stock* to exercise the option. You have immature ISO stock if you acquired the stock by exercising an incentive stock option and haven't yet satisfied the special ISO holding period (the later of two years after option grant or one year after exercise). If you're *not* using immature ISO stock to pay for the shares you're buying, the shares you're using can be any of the following:

- *Mature* ISO stock (in other words, stock you acquired by exercising an incentive stock option long enough ago that you've satisfied the special ISO holding period).

- Stock from exercising nonqualified stock options.

- Stock acquired in any other way, including purchases on the open market.

Using Shares Other than Immature ISO Shares

Generally, if you're going to use stock to exercise an ISO, you want to use shares *other than* immature ISO stock. Here are the *regular tax* consequences when you do so:

- For regular tax purposes, you don't report any income on the exercise of the incentive stock option. (This rule is the same as if you used cash to exercise your option.)

- You don't report any gain or loss on the shares you used to pay the purchase price on the option. That's because you've made a tax-free exchange of those shares for ISO shares.

- The shares you receive are divided into two batches. One batch includes a number of shares equal to the number of shares you turned in (the *exchange shares*). The other group includes all the additional shares you received (the *added shares*).

- The exchange shares have the same basis as the shares you turned in. They also have the same holding period as the shares you turned in—but only for purposes of determining whether any capital gain or loss on a sale is long-term. For purposes of determining whether you've satisfied the special ISO holding period, your holding period for these shares begins on the date you exercise the option.

- The added shares have a basis equal to the amount of cash (if any) you paid to exercise the option. This amount may be zero or close to zero because you used stock to pay most or all of the exercise price. These shares have a holding period that begins on the date you exercised the option.

- Both the exchange shares and the added shares are subject to the rules that cause you to report compensation income if you make a *disqualifying disposition* before satisfying the special ISO holding period.

There are some quirks in the way the rules for disqualifying dispositions apply after you use stock to exercise an ISO. See Chapter 27 for details.

AMT consequences. The IRS hasn't spelled out the consequences under the alternative minimum tax in as great detail as the regular tax consequences. The following results would be consistent with the approach the IRS has taken in this area:

- When you use stock to exercise an ISO, you have to report an AMT adjustment in the same amount as if you had used cash to exercise the option.

- The exchange shares have the same AMT basis as the shares you used to pay the exercise price.

- The added shares have an AMT basis equal to the amount of cash you paid (if any) *plus* the amount of the AMT adjustment.

The significance of AMT basis is explained in Chapter 33.

Using Immature ISO Shares

Because of a special rule—sometimes called the *anti-pyramid rule*—it's generally undesirable to use immature ISO stock to exercise an incentive stock option. Here are the consequences:

- For regular income tax purposes, you don't report any income on the exercise of the new ISO.

- However, *you've made a disqualifying disposition of the immature ISO stock you turned in.* That means you have to report compensation income equal to the bargain element from the exercise of the *old* ISO (the one you exercised to acquire the immature ISO stock). You can't reduce the amount you report as compensation income even if the stock has declined in value since the date of the previous option exercise.

- At the same time, the disposition of the immature ISO stock is treated in part as a tax-free exchange. So apart from the compensation income you report as described above, you don't report gain or loss on the exchange of old ISO shares for new ISO shares, even if the stock has gone up in value since the previous option exercise.

- The shares you receive are divided into two groups. One group includes a number of shares equal to the number of shares you turned in (the *exchange shares*). The other group includes all the additional shares you received (the *added shares*).

- The exchange shares have the same basis as the shares you turned in, increased by the amount of compensation income reported because of the disqualifying disposition. They also have the same holding period as the shares you turned in—but only for purposes of determining whether any capital gain or loss on a sale is long-term. For purposes of determining whether you've satisfied the special ISO holding period, your holding period for these shares begins on the date you exercise the new ISO.

- The added shares have a basis equal to the amount of cash (if any) paid to exercise the option. This may be zero or close to zero because you used stock to pay most or all of the exercise price. These shares have a holding period that begins on the date you exercised the new ISO.

- Both the exchange shares and the added shares are subject to the rules that require you to report compensation income if you make a disqualifying disposition.

See Chapter 27 for a discussion of early disposition after using stock to exercise an ISO.

AMT consequences. The following description of alternative minimum tax consequences would be consistent with the approach the IRS has taken in this area:

- You have to report an AMT adjustment on the exercise of the new ISO in the same amount as if you had used cash to exercise the option.

- The exchange shares have the same AMT basis as the shares you used to pay the exercise price. (The AMT basis of the shares you used to pay the exercise price already included the bargain element from exercise of the original ISO.)

- The added shares have an AMT basis equal to the amount of cash you paid (if any) *plus* the amount of the AMT adjustment.

The significance of AMT basis is explained in Chapter 33.

Chapter 27
Early Disposition After Stock Exercise

Chapter 26 describes the tax consequences of using stock to exercise an incentive stock option. Yet it doesn't describe the tax consequences of an early disposition of shares after using stock to exercise an ISO. As it turns out, this is a tricky little puzzle, and certain interpretations of the rule here could work in your favor—or against you.

> **Steep climbing.** This chapter contains expert analysis that many readers will find difficult.

Overview

It's easier to see the issues if we have a set of facts in front of us:

> **Example:** You have an ISO that lets you buy 600 shares at $5 per share (total exercise price of $3,000). The stock is currently trading at $12. You already own 250 shares you bought on the open market at $10. At the current price of $12 per share, the 250 shares you already own are worth $3,000, the exercise price for the option. So you use these shares to exercise the option, surrendering 250 shares as "payment" and getting back 600 shares. Before satisfying the special holding period, you sell the stock at $14.

How much compensation income do you report? At first blush, the answer is obvious. You bought 600 shares worth $7,200 for $3,000, so the bargain element at the time you exercised the option was $4,200. The stock hasn't gone down since you exercised; in fact, it went up. It would seem you have to report $4,200 of compensation income.

On closer inspection, that may not be the correct answer. When you sell immature ISO stock to an unrelated person, you report compensation income equal to the *lesser* of the bargain element on that stock or the amount of gain you have on that sale. You have two different batches of shares now: the *exchange* shares (with a basis of $10 per share) and the *additional* shares (with zero basis). That means you have a different amount of gain per share on the two different batches of shares.

Your *bargain element* was $7 per share because the option price was $5 and the value of the stock was $12. Yet your *gain* on the exchange shares is only $4 per share. One possible conclusion is that you report $4 per share of compensation income on the exchange shares. You have more than $7 of gain on the additional shares because they have zero basis. Yet the amount of compensation income you report on those shares is limited to the bargain element of $7 per share.

This isn't the only possible interpretation of the rules. It seems to be consistent with the proposed regulations, however. I'm not aware of any authority that would indicate that it's incorrect.

How You Can Benefit

You may be able to benefit from this quirk in the rules—assuming you're willing to take the risk that the IRS won't agree with this interpretation. Suppose you're planning to exercise an ISO and you intend to dispose of all of the stock right away. Instead of using cash to exercise the option, you buy stock at the current market price and use this stock to pay the exercise price. In the example above, you would buy 250 shares at $12 and immediately use them to pay the exercise price on the 600 shares. Then you sell all the shares at $12.

Result? You have no alternative minimum tax (AMT) because you disposed of the stock in the same year you exercised the option. You report no gain, and no compensation income, on the exchange shares. With respect to the additional shares, you report $7 per share of compensation income and $5 per share short-term capital gain.

You're still reporting the same overall amount of income as if you used cash to exercise the option. The difference is that part of that income is converted from compensation income to short-term capital gain. In many situations short-term capital gain ends up being taxed at the same rate as ordinary income—but that's not always true. If you happen to have capital losses that would otherwise be unused, or short-term losses that would otherwise offset long-term gains, this maneuver can lower your taxes.

A Step Further

We can take this a step further. Suppose you're only going to dispose of *some* of the shares after you exercise your ISO. It's tempting to think that you can be way ahead of the game if you sell the exchange shares and continue to hold the additional shares. That way, the shares you're selling first are the shares that produce zero gain and zero compensation income. You can continue to hold the additional shares until they qualify for long-term capital gain treatment, avoiding the need to report compensation income altogether, even though you sold some shares at the same time you exercised the option.

This sounds almost too good to be true, and indeed there's a catch. If you're a brave soul, you won't let this catch deter you.

The proposed regulations say that when you sell shares after using stock to exercise an ISO, you have to sell the shares with the lowest basis first. If that rule prevails, you're actually worse off on a partial sale than you would be if you used cash to exercise the option. Your partial sale would come out of the additional shares that have zero basis, and you would report compensation income *and* short-term capital gain on the sale. That's not a good result, when you could have used cash to exercise your option and reported only compensation income.

The reason you might forge ahead anyway is that this rule appears only in *proposed* regulations. Proposed regulations aren't binding on the IRS—or on you. And outside of the proposed regulations there's nothing to say you can't sell the exchange shares first. On the contrary, there's a long-established procedure under which you're permitted to identify which shares you're selling if you sell less than all of the shares you hold (see Chapter 43).

If you take this approach and the IRS figures it out, they probably won't like it. You could end up with a dispute on your hands, and even if you win, the cost of the dispute may eat up much of your tax savings. *Caveat lector!*

Another Source of Pain

Finally, you should be aware that there's another potential source of pain when you use stock to exercise an ISO and then have a disqualifying disposition. Let's go back to our original example where the exercise price was $5 and the stock was worth $12 when you exercised. Suppose the price of the stock goes *down* after you exercise. To make things simple, let's say it goes all the way down to $5, and then you sell the stock.

At that price, you have no gain at all from your ISO. If you had used cash to exercise your ISO, you would have no gain on the sale. Yet when you use stock to exercise the ISO, you end up with some stock that has zero basis. Even at $5 per share, you have a gain on sale of this stock, and that gain would be reported as compensation income. You would have capital loss on the other shares, but you may not get full value from that deduction. Overall, you may end up with a tax cost even though you have zero profit.

Chapter 28
Deferring Income from Nonqualified Options

A provocative question: *Can I exercise my nonqualified options without reporting income?* No one knows for sure whether you can or not. There's a theory that you can, if you're willing to take some risk. The idea here is not to avoid reporting income altogether, but to delay it until a later year.

Words of Caution

The idea for deferring income from nonqualified options has been around for a few years. Some experts in this area believe it works; others aren't so sure. The IRS is aware of this planning technique but so far hasn't taken a position on it. There's no question some people are using it, but that doesn't mean it's completely safe.

In any case, this technique isn't available to everyone. Your company must be willing to set up the appropriate arrangements, and you need to own stock that can be used to exercise your option.

How It Works

The theory for this deferral technique is based on the bifurcated treatment that applies if you use stock to pay the purchase price when you exercise a nonqualified option. As Chapter 25 explains, in this situation you end up with two batches of stock. One batch, which I call the *exchange shares*, is considered to be received in a tax-free exchange for the old shares you used to buy the stock. The other batch, which I call the *added shares*, represent your income from exercising the option.

Now suppose your employer offers you an opportunity to turn in enough old shares to exercise your option without receiving the full number of shares to which you're entitled. Instead of receiving exchange shares and added shares, you'll receive exchange shares and a right to future income. The idea is that you have no income from receiving the exchange shares, because that's a tax-free exchange—and you won't have to report income from the added shares because you don't receive them. Instead, you'll report income when you actually receive the deferred income.

> **Example:** Six months before you actually exercise your nonqualified option, you notify your employer that you want to receive deferred income rather than added shares when you use shares to exercise the option. After waiting six months, you turn in enough shares to exercise the option and receive the same number of shares in return: the *exchange* shares. You don't report any income or gain on the exchange.
>
> In addition, you receive a right to a cash payment at some specified point in the future—say, ten years from now. Until then, the amount of the deferred payment will be adjusted to provide you with some kind of market return, which could be interest at the prime rate or a return based on the performance of a stock index, for example. When the 10 years are up, you receive (and report as compensation income) a cash payment equal to the deferred amount with the investment return.

Notice that you have to notify the employer six months ahead of time if you want to take advantage of this deferral arrangement. No one knows for sure that the six-month period is long enough to make you safe, or that you couldn't use a shorter period. Some experts might suggest that you have to give this notice six months ahead of time *and* in the preceding year. The point of this requirement is to defeat a possible argument of the IRS that you have *constructive receipt* of the income when you exercise the option, because you had a choice at that time (or shortly before that time) to receive current income or deferred income.

Another point: your deferred income is *vested* (you won't lose it if your employment terminates)—but it isn't *secured*. If the company encounters financial difficulties and is unable to pay all its debts, the amount owed to *you* may be one of the debts that goes unpaid.

Evaluation

The tax issues involved in determining whether this technique works are somewhat theoretical. There's some tax risk in using this approach, and credit risk as well. Furthermore, you can't use this approach unless the company is willing to set up the necessary arrangements. There are a variety of good reasons why a company may not want to do so. If the company does want to pursue this approach, it's important to have it structured by an expert familiar with this type of arrangement, to provide the most favorable structure and advise on the risks.

Chapter 29
Reload Options

A twist on options that began appearing in the late 1980's has been steadily gaining popularity. In these arrangements, when you use stock to exercise options, you get new options for each share of stock you surrendered. Your new option may be called a restoration or replacement option. An option that permits you to receive a replacement option is called a *reload option*.

How They Work

If your option has a reload feature, it generally applies only if you use stock to exercise the option. For each share you turn in, you receive a new option priced at the current value of the stock. Usually the new option expires at the same time the old one would have expired.

> **Example:** You hold an option to buy 1,000 shares of your company's stock at $12 per share. The stock is currently trading at $16. You exercise the option, paying the purchase price with 750 shares of stock you already own. You receive 1,000 shares (increasing your total by 250) plus a new option to buy 750 shares at $16 per share.

Without the reload feature, you would simply receive 1,000 shares. That's certainly a benefit: you own 250 more shares than you did before you exercised the option. But the reload feature gives you something more: a new option that allows you to profit from further appreciation in the value of the company's stock.

Other Terms

There's no standard way to provide reload options. If you receive such an option, it's important to read the agreement carefully to understand exactly how it works. Here are some of the possible provisions:

- The reload feature may apply only when you use shares you've owned for a specified period of time, or it may apply only when you use shares you previously acquired under the company's stock option plan.

- You may have to wait a specified period of time before exercising the reload option, or be limited in the number of times you can get reloads. Sometimes the replacement option doesn't include a reload feature, so you only get one bite at the apple.

Tax Consequences

The tax consequences of reload options are no different from the tax consequences of options without this feature. You don't report income of any kind when you receive an option from your company. Receiving a new option when you exercise the old one is certainly a valuable benefit, but it doesn't affect your taxes until you exercise the replacement option.

Strategy

You might think that reload options involve some complicated strategies. According to a 1999 academic study, the optimal strategy for exercising these options is very simple: exercise as often as possible, provided that the option is *in the money* (in other words, the value of the stock is higher than the exercise price of the option). Exercising the option gives you an opportunity to lock in some or all of your existing profit while preserving the ability to obtain more profit if the stock continues to rise in value.

This study made some assumptions that may not apply to your reload option, and did not take into account the tax consequences of exercising the option. There may be cases where this simple strategy isn't the right one. Still, you should probably start from the premise that this is the best course of action, and then consider whether there are valid reasons not to follow it.

Controversy

Reload options are somewhat controversial, with some people saying they are too generous, and don't represent good compensation policy. I wonder whether the critics truly understand the program. In particular, they may be overlooking two points that put reload options in perspective.

The first is that a reload option, although more valuable than an option without this feature, has a *maximum* value equal to the value of the number of shares of stock the initial option permits you to buy. That's true no matter how many times it reloads or how long it extends into the future. It's simply a mathematical fact that you can't wring more value from a reload option than you would get from owning that number of shares.

The other point is that the maximum number of shares the company can end up issuing under all the exercises of a repeating reload option is equal to the number of shares you can buy under the original option. For example, if you start with an option to buy 100 shares, and you exercise by turning in 80 shares, you get 20 new shares and an option for another 80. The company has issued 20 shares, and now has an option outstanding for 80. The total is still 100, and always will be.

Reload options may sound like some magical pyramid scheme, but they're not. They provide significant value to the holders, but the cost to the company is limited, just as it is for traditional options.

Chapter 30
"Early Exercise" Stock Option Plans

For many years it has been more or less standard for stock option plans, or the options issued under such plans, to provide for staged exercise of options. In a typical arrangement, you have to wait a year before you can exercise any of your options. At the end of a year, you can exercise 25%, then another year later you qualify to exercise another 25% and so on.

Recently a different approach has gained popularity, especially with startup companies that are planning to go public. These arrangements permit you to exercise all your options immediately. If you do that, however, your stock isn't vested right away. You'll forfeit it (or sell it back to the company at your original purchase price) if your employment terminates within a specified time. Vesting of the stock may be staged in a manner similar to the exercise of options under a more traditional plan—say, 25% per year over four years. I call these plans *early exercise* stock option plans.

These plans have unique tax consequences. There are no regulations or rulings that spell out the details with certainty. The following description is consistent with positions the IRS has taken in private rulings, proposed regulations and instructions to Form 6251.

Section 83b Election

Early exercise plans are designed to permit you to exercise options at a time when the stock you receive won't be *vested*. Unless you file the section 83b election, you'll report income at the time the stock vests. More importantly, the *amount* of income you report will be based on the value of the stock when it vests. If the value of the stock goes up rapidly between the time you exercise the option and the time the stock vests, you'll report a great deal of compensation income on the vesting date.

> Part VIII of this book deals with the subject of vesting in general, and the section 83b election in particular.

These plans are designed with the idea that you may want to exercise the option before the stock has gone up very much—perhaps even immediately after you receive the option. And the expectation is that you'll file the section 83b election. The plan or the option may even *require* you to file the section 83b election when you exercise. That way, you report income at the time you exercise the option—and you won't be hit with a huge tax liability when the stock vests.

Example: You received a nonqualified option to buy 10,000 shares at $0.50 when the company is in its infancy. Now things are looking good. The stock's value is $1, but it will zoom to $5 if the company secures venture capital. In another 18 months the company may go public, and the stock could be at $20 or higher. That would give you a profit of close to $200,000.

If you don't exercise until the stock is at $20, all that profit will be compensation income, taxed at the highest rates. Even if you exercise now, you may have to report most of your profit as compensation income if you don't make the section 83b election. But if you exercise now and make the election, you report only $5,000 of compensation income. Any future growth in the value of the stock will be capital gain. If you hold the stock more than a year, your capital gain will qualify for the favorable long-term rates. Potential tax savings: as much as $40,000 or more.

Special Section 83b Election

There's a little twist on these rules if your option is an incentive stock option, rather than a nonqualified stock option. This type of plan permits you to exercise your option at a time when the stock you receive isn't vested. The fact that your stock isn't vested has no bearing on your regular income tax. You don't report income when you exercise an ISO, whether the stock is vested or not. Yet it's important that the stock isn't vested—and it may be important for you to do something about it.

Under the alternative minimum tax, exercise of an incentive stock option is treated the same as exercise on a nonqualified option. Under the regular tax, if you exercise a nonqualified option but the stock isn't vested, you don't report income at that time. You report income when the stock vests instead. The same principle applies to AMT treatment of exercise of an ISO.

At first blush that sounds like a good thing. AMT is bad, so why not put it off until another year? The problem here is the same as the problem with nonqualified options under the regular tax. When you postpone the *income* from exercising your option, you also postpone the *measurement* of that income.

> **Example:** Suppose you have an ISO to buy stock at $5 per share. When you exercise the option, the stock is valued at $6 per share. If the stock is vested at that time, you report an AMT adjustment of $1 per share. But let's assume the stock doesn't vest until a year later. During that time the company has gone public and the stock is worth $30 per share when it vests. Now you have to report an AMT adjustment of $25 per share. If you have a large number of shares, that's a big difference!

In dealing with nonqualified options under the regular tax, you can file a *section 83b election* in this situation. You tell the IRS you want to ignore the fact that the stock isn't vested. You'll pay the tax now, and take your chances on possibly forfeiting the stock before it vests. In the example above, if you had a nonqualified option and filed the section 83b election, you would report income of $1 per share when you exercise the option and nothing at all when the stock vests.

As it turns out, you can do the same thing under the AMT if you exercise an incentive stock option when the stock isn't vested. You'll file a *special* section 83b election just for purposes of the AMT. The election will work exactly the same way for the AMT as the regular section 83b election works under the regular tax. You'll report your AMT adjustment in the year you exercise the option, even though the stock won't vest until later. The amount of the adjustment will be determined as of the exercise date. You won't have anything to report at the time the stock vests.

There may be some risk in making this election if you paid substantially less than fair market value when you used the ISO to buy the stock. You could end up paying tax sooner than necessary, and even paying *more* tax than necessary.

The election can produce huge benefits in some cases, however. The earlier example illustrates such a situation. The AMT adjustment at the time of exercise is very small, so there's very little cost in making the election. Meanwhile, the company is planning to go public, with the possibility of a big increase in the value of the stock— and a big increase in the adjustment you report when the stock vests if you don't make the election.

Exercise Immediately?

Early exercise stock option plans invite you to consider the possibility of exercising your option immediately after you receive it. If you do this, your compensation income (or AMT adjustment) should be close to zero, because the exercise price is equal to fair market value at the time the option was granted. You can file the section 83b election (or special section 83b election) described above to avoid having to report any compensation income or AMT adjustment at the time the stock vests. If everything works right, you'll received the full value of your option while reporting nothing but long-term capital gain. This is why early exercise plans are attractive to some companies, especially ones that are planning to go public.

Sound too good to be true? It isn't, really. To see why, think about what would have happened if your company offered you a different deal. Instead of an option, the company simply said you're allowed to buy some stock right now, paying fair market value, with the stock subject to restrictions so that it isn't vested. This is the type of deal that's described in Chapter 9. You would make the (regular) section 83b election to avoid having to report income when the stock vests. The election doesn't cost you anything because you paid full fair market value for the stock. Guess what? You would be in exactly the same situation as if you exercised an option under an early exercise stock option plan.

There really isn't any magic with this type of plan. In effect, if you exercise immediately you're giving up the benefit of holding an option: the ability to wait and see how the stock performs before exercising. For a mature company with stock price established on the market, you wouldn't be interested in such an arrangement. You'd be better off buying the stock on the open market without any restriction.

The payoff comes with a company that isn't publicly traded. You don't have any way to buy the stock on the market because it isn't available. The only way you can get it is if the company offers you a deal. Getting the kind of a deal described here shortly before the company goes public can be a major bonanza. That's how Margaret Whitman of eBay, Inc. put herself in a position to save over $100 million in taxes!

Of course you don't *have* to exercise your options immediately. Particularly if there's some doubt as to whether the company can pull off an IPO (or anything else that will make its value go up), you may want to wait and see. That's the benefit of an option: the ability to get a free look. There's a tax cost if you wait until after the value has gone up a great deal, though, so the "look" isn't completely free.

Part VII
Alternative Minimum Tax (AMT)

The alternative minimum tax affects a small but growing percentage of taxpayers. When it applies, the cost can be substantial. What's worse, this tax is so complicated that it's often difficult to predict when it will apply. Recipients of equity compensation have a particular interest in AMT because of two situations that bring it into play: exercise of incentive stock options, and large long-term capital gains.

There is some good news associated with AMT. In many cases you can recover some or all of your AMT as a credit against your regular tax in a later year. To take full advantage, you have to understand *dual basis* as well as the credit itself.

Part VII
Alternative Minimum Tax

Chapter 31
Overview of AMT

The basic idea behind the alternative minimum tax is a good one: people with very high levels of income shouldn't be able to completely avoid paying income tax while the rest of us pony up each year. The AMT is a poor reflection of that idea, however. Many high-income individuals escape its reach—and every year it ensnares more and more people who were never intended to be affected.

Whatever its merits or demerits, the AMT is a potential problem you have to deal with if you receive equity compensation. It's of particular interest to people who have incentive stock options because exercise of ISOs very frequently brings AMT into play. And it isn't just a matter of paying tax when you exercise your ISOs. You also have to understand the consequences when you sell the stock you acquired by exercising the options.

We'll see that the AMT can also apply if you have a large long-term capital gain. That means you can get hit with AMT even if you never had an incentive stock option. If you used nonqualified options to acquire stock that went up in value after you acquired it, for example, you could end up with a large long-term capital gain—and an AMT problem.

Overview

The alternative minimum tax is an extra tax some people have to pay on top of the regular income tax. The original idea behind this tax was to prevent people with very high incomes from using deductions, exclusions and credits to pay little or no tax. For various reasons, though, the AMT reaches more people each year, including some people who don't have lots of special tax benefits. Congress is studying ways to correct this problem, but until it does, almost anyone is a potential target for this tax.

The name comes from the way the tax works. The AMT provides an *alternative* set of rules for calculating your income tax. In theory these rules determine a *minimum* amount of tax that someone with your income should be required to pay. If you're already paying at least that much because of the "regular" income tax, you don't have to pay AMT. But if your regular tax falls below this minimum, you have to make up the difference by paying alternative minimum tax.

Q: How do I know if I have to worry about the AMT?

A: Unfortunately, there's no good answer to this common question—which is one of the big problems with the AMT. You can have AMT liability because of one big item on your tax return, or because of a combination of many small items. Some things that can contribute to AMT liability are very mundane items that appear on many tax returns, such as a deduction for state income tax or interest on a second mortgage, or even your personal and dependency exemptions. There's a list of such items later in this chapter. If you use computer software to prepare your tax return, the program should be able to do the AMT calculation. If you're preparing a return by hand, the only way to know for sure is to fill out Form 6251—a laborious process.

There are two essential pieces to the AMT. First, you need to understand how your *AMT liability* is calculated for a year when you pay AMT. And second, you need to know how the *AMT credit* can reduce your taxes in years *after* the year you paid alternative minimum tax.

AMT Liability

The best way to understand alternative minimum tax liability is to see how it's calculated. Here's the big picture.

Compute an alternate tax. First, you figure the amount of tax you would owe under a different set of income tax rules. What's different about these rules? Broadly speaking, three things:

- Various tax benefits that are available under the regular income tax are reduced or eliminated.

- You get a special deduction called the *AMT exemption*, which is designed to prevent the AMT from applying to taxpayers with modest income. This deduction *phases out* when your income reaches higher levels, a fact that causes significant problems under the alternative minimum tax.

- You calculate the tax using AMT rates, which start at 26% and move to 28% at higher income levels. By comparison, the regular tax rates start at 15% and then move through a series of steps to a high of 39.6%.

The result of this calculation is the amount of income tax you would owe under the "alternative" system of tax.

Compare with the regular tax. Then you compare this tax with your regular income tax. If the regular income tax is *higher*, you don't owe any AMT. If the regular income tax is lower than the AMT calculation, though, the difference between the two taxes is the amount of AMT you have to pay.

Example 1: Your regular income tax is $47,000. When you calculate your tax using the AMT rules, you come up with $39,000. That's lower than the regular tax, so you don't pay any AMT.

Example 2: Your regular income tax is $47,000. When you calculate your tax using the AMT rules, you come up with $58,000. You have to pay $11,000 of AMT on top of $47,000 of regular income tax.

If you're paying attention, you've probably noticed that the total amount of tax you pay in Example 2 is equal to the tax calculated under the AMT: $58,000. But it's important to note that you actually pay $47,000 of regular tax plus $11,000 of AMT, as we'll see below.

Reporting and paying the tax. To calculate and report your AMT liability you need to fill out *Form 6251, Alternative Minimum Tax—Individuals.* The instructions for that form are very useful, particularly because the IRS discontinued the publication it used to put out on the AMT.

> You're required to take your AMT liability into account in determining how much estimated tax you pay. See Chapter 42 on estimated tax.

AMT Credit

Here's good news: a portion of your AMT liability—perhaps all—may reduce the tax you owe on future tax returns. Whether you receive the AMT credit depends in part on the type of items that gave rise to your AMT liability, and in part on your tax calculation for the year in which you claim the credit. See Chapter 34 for details.

Top Ten Things that Cause AMT Liability

Here's a list of items that can cause (or contribute to) liability under the alternative minimum tax. The list isn't *complete*—there are still other items that can contribute to AMT liability. Based on my experience, the items described below are likely to affect more people than the other items. For a complete list, see IRS Form 6251 and the accompanying instructions. By the way, if you count more than 10 items below, just consider it a bonus.

Exemptions. Believe it or not, personal exemptions contribute to AMT liability. The exemptions you claim for yourself, your spouse and your dependents are not allowed when calculating alternative minimum tax. If you have a large number of exemptions, you may run into AMT liability even without taking any of the special tax breaks the AMT was originally aimed at.

> A taxpayer with a large number of exemptions challenged the AMT in court, saying Congress didn't intend for the tax to apply to someone in his situation. But the law is clear, and the court ruled for the IRS.

Standard deduction. Some 70% of American taxpayers claim the standard deduction (rather than itemizing). The standard deduction isn't allowed under the AMT. Usually this isn't a problem because the AMT generally hits people with higher incomes, and these people are more likely to claim itemized deductions. Yet it's worth noting that a deduction that's so widely used can contribute to AMT liability.

State and local taxes. If you itemize, there's a good chance you claim a deduction for state and local tax, including property tax and state income tax. These deductions are not allowed under the AMT. If you live in a place where state and local taxes are high, you're more likely to pay alternative minimum tax.

Interest on second mortgages. The AMT allows a deduction for interest on mortgage borrowings used to buy, build or improve your principal residence. If you borrowed against your home for some other purpose, the interest deduction may be allowed under the regular income tax but won't be allowed under the alternative minimum tax.

Medical expenses. Yes, medical expenses. The AMT allows a medical expense deduction, but it's more limited than the deduction under the regular income tax. If you claim an itemized deduction for medical expenses, part or all of it will be disallowed when you calculate your alternative minimum tax.

Miscellaneous itemized deductions. Certain itemized deductions are available if your total in this general category is more than 2% of your adjusted gross income. Among the items here are unreimbursed employee expenses, tax preparation fees, and many investment expenses. You can't deduct these items under the AMT, though. If you claim a large number in this area, you could end up paying alternative minimum tax.

Various credits. Many of the credits that are allowed when you calculate your regular income tax aren't allowed when you calculate your AMT. The more credits you claim, the more likely it is that you'll end up paying alternative minimum tax.

> Congress acted in 1998, and again in 1999, to prevent various "personal credits" from causing AMT liability. The relief covered some old credits (such as the dependent care credit) and new ones (the child credit and the education credit). This was a quick fix, and expires in 2001. Further action is required to extend this relief to 2002 and later years.

Incentive stock options. As detailed in Part V of this book, you have to report an AMT adjustment when you exercise an incentive stock option. Exercising a large ISO is almost certain to cause you to pay alternative minimum tax.

Long-term capital gains. Long-term capital gains receive the same preferential rate under the AMT as they do under the regular income tax. In theory, they shouldn't cause you to pay alternative minimum tax. In practice, it's possible to be stuck with AMT liability because of a large capital gain, as explained in Chapter 32.

Tax-exempt interest. Interest that's exempt from the regular income tax may or may not be exempt from the AMT. It depends on complicated rules that are fully understood only by bond lawyers. Bonds that aren't exempt from AMT pay a slightly higher rate of interest to compensate for the fact that they aren't fully tax-exempt. If you invest in bonds that aren't exempt under the alternative minimum tax, you're a candidate for AMT liability.

Many mutual funds that provide exempt interest invest at least *some* of their money in bonds that aren't exempt under the AMT, to get a higher rate of interest. Their annual statement tells you how much of your income is taxable under the alternative minimum tax.

Tax shelters. The Tax Reform Act of 1986 severely curtailed the ability of most people to reduce their income tax through tax shelters. Yet there are still some legitimate ways of reducing tax liabilities through investments in certain types of partnership arrangements involving such activities as oil and gas drilling. The AMT provides reduced tax benefits for these activities. You should always explore alternative minimum tax consequences (among other things) before investing in a tax shelter.

Chapter 32
AMT and Long-Term Capital Gain

Congress didn't intend for the alternative minimum tax to apply merely because you have a long-term capital gain. When Congress reduced the capital gain rates in 1997, it provided that the lower rates would apply under the AMT, too. But the way it works out, you may still pay AMT because of a large long-term capital gain.

The AMT Exemption

A major reason for paying AMT in the year of a large capital gain is the *AMT exemption.* This is a special deduction that's designed to prevent the alternative minimum tax from applying at lower income levels. The problem is that the AMT exemption is *phased out* when your income goes above a certain level. Capital gain is income, so it can reduce or eliminate your AMT exemption.

For example, if you're single and your income under the AMT rules is $112,500 or less, you're allowed an AMT exemption of $33,750. Normally that's enough to prevent you from paying AMT unless you're able to claim special tax benefits that reduce your regular tax. But suppose your income is around that level before you add a $150,000 capital gain (which could come from sale of stock you acquired by exercising an option you received as compensation). Your tax on the capital gain is 20% under both the regular tax and the AMT: $30,000. Under the AMT, though, the added income wiped out your AMT exemption.

How big is the effect? At this level, your AMT rate is 26%. The $33,750 exemption reduces the tax under the AMT calculation by $8,775. In these facts, the regular tax on this gain is $30,000 and the AMT is $38,775, which comes partly from phasing out the AMT exemption.

That doesn't mean you pay $8,775 of AMT in this situation. Most people have at least a little bit of a cushion between the amount of regular tax they pay and the level where they would have to start paying alternative minimum tax. (The size of your cushion depends on various items, including those listed in the previous chapter.) Besides, the capital gain can cause some tax benefits to phase out under the regular tax, too. But there's a good chance someone in this situation would pay several thousand dollars of AMT.

> During 1998, President Clinton's blind trust sold some assets, causing him to have a large long-term capital gain and incur alternative minimum tax liability.

Selling ISO Stock

As we'll see in the next chapter, you get an AMT adjustment in your favor when you sell stock acquired by exercising an incentive stock option. Normally this adjustment helps you qualify for the AMT credit. Yet the capital gain effect described in this chapter may work in the opposite direction, making it difficult for you to use the entire credit when you sell your ISO stock.

More Bad News

There's more bad news. People who get caught by the AMT because of a large long-term capital gain usually don't qualify for the AMT credit in later years. The AMT liability is being caused by items that aren't considered *timing* items. Possibly you have some timing items *in addition to* the long-term capital gain, and in that case at least part of your AMT would be available as a credit in later years. More often, this added tax is just a dead loss.

What to Do

In many cases there isn't a heck of a lot you can do about this added tax. But if you're aware of the issue, you may be able to take measures to reduce the impact.

Timing your capital gains. In some situations you can control the year in which you report capital gains. You may be able to delay a sale until after the end of the year, or spread the gain over a number of years by using an installment sale. There's no simple answer to whether these measures help or hurt, so someone has to sharpen a pencil and grind out the numbers.

For example, your gain may be at a level where spreading it over a number of years will keep you out of the AMT—or at least reduce the impact. In this case an installment sale might be an attractive alternative. But suppose your gain is so large that it will phase out your AMT exemption amount many times over. In this situation, you may get a better result by reporting all the gain in one year, so you're only affecting one year's exemption amount.

Timing other items. Another way to plan for the AMT is to see if you can change the timing of other items that are affected by the alternative minimum tax. For example, if you make estimated payments of state income tax, you may try to schedule your payments so they don't fall in the same year as your large capital gain. If that means delaying your state estimates to an extent that causes you to incur a penalty, you'll have to compare the amount of that penalty with the tax savings under the AMT.

Chapter 33
AMT and Dual Basis Assets

Your *basis* in an asset, such as stock or real property, is used to determine how much gain or loss you report when you sell that asset. In some situations an asset may have one basis for regular income tax purposes and a different basis (usually higher) for alternative minimum tax purposes. When that happens, the AMT gain or loss on a sale of that asset won't be the same as the regular tax gain or loss. If you're not alert to this situation you may end up needlessly paying more tax than required.

What Causes Dual Basis

Ordinarily, your basis for an asset is simply the amount you paid for it plus any costs of acquisition (such as brokerage fees). But various events can cause an adjustment in the basis of an asset. For example, if you claim a deduction for depreciation of an asset, you reduce your basis in that asset by the amount of the deduction.

Some of the things that cause an adjustment in basis under the regular tax have a different treatment under the alternative minimum tax. For example, you may have to use a less favorable depreciation schedule for AMT purposes than you use for the regular tax. That means you've claimed smaller depreciation deductions for that asset under the AMT, and as a consequence will have a higher basis in the asset.

> **Example:** Over the years you've used a piece of equipment that cost $20,000, you've claimed depreciation deductions of $12,000, leaving you with an *adjusted basis* of $8,000. During those same years, your AMT depreciation deductions for

the same piece of equipment were $9,000. That means your AMT basis is $11,000.

Incentive Stock Options

One very important circumstance where you can have dual basis in an asset is when you exercise an incentive stock option. You have to report an *adjustment* for AMT purposes when you exercise an incentive stock option. As a result you may end up paying alternative minimum tax. But another result is that your AMT basis in the stock is increased by the amount of the adjustment.

> **Example:** At a time when your company's stock was trading at $80 per share, you exercised an incentive stock option to purchase 500 shares at $24 per share. For AMT purposes you report an adjustment of $28,000 ($56 per share). The result is that you hold stock with a basis of $24 per share for regular tax purposes and $80 per share for AMT purposes.

Sale of Dual Basis Asset

When you sell a dual basis asset, you report the difference between the regular tax gain or loss and the AMT gain or loss as an adjustment on Form 6251. *If your AMT basis is higher (as is usually the case), you report this item as a negative adjustment.* The result may be to reduce the amount of AMT you pay or increase the amount of AMT credit you can use.

> **Example:** In the preceding example, you held stock with a basis of $24 per share for regular tax purposes and $80 per share for AMT purposes. When you sell the stock for $90 per share, your gain is $66 per share for regular tax purposes but only $10 per share under the alternative minimum tax. On line 9 of Form 6251, you'll report a favorable adjustment of $56 per share on your AMT calculation. If you have to pay AMT in the

year of the sale, this adjustment will reduce your alternative minimum tax liability. If you don't have to pay alternative minimum tax in the year of the sale, the adjustment may make it possible to claim a larger portion of your AMT credit in that year.

AMT Capital Loss Limitation

Before you can claim an adjustment for dual basis under the AMT, you have to refigure your overall capital gain or loss for AMT purposes. You fill out (but don't file) a new Schedule D showing gain or loss as determined under the AMT rules. If the result is an overall loss greater than $3,000, your AMT adjustment will be limited.

Example: You exercise an ISO at a time when the spread is $90,000, paying $25,000 in AMT in the year of exercise. The following year you sell the stock after a $50,000 decline in value. For regular tax purposes, you still have a gain of $40,000. Under the AMT, though, you have a loss of $50,000. Assuming no other capital gains or losses, your adjustment would be $43,000. That's the difference between the regular tax gain of $40,000 and the allowable AMT capital loss of $3,000. The remaining AMT loss carries over to the following year: an *AMT capital loss carryforward.*

Chapter 34
AMT Credit

You don't have to be quite so sad (or mad) about paying alternative minimum tax if you can get some or all of it back as a credit in a later year. That's exactly what happens in many cases—but not all. It pays to understand the AMT credit.

Credit Against Regular Income Tax

You can't use the AMT credit to reduce your AMT liability. Instead, you use it against your *regular* income tax liability. It's called the AMT credit because it arises from paying alternative minimum tax in a prior year.

Calculating the Credit

Working with the AMT credit is a two-step process. First you find out how much credit is *available*, then you find out how much of the available credit you can *use*.

Find the available credit. The first part of your task is to find out how much of the AMT liability from a *prior* year is *eligible* for the credit. This involves recalculating the alternative minimum tax under a special set of rules—sort of an *alternative* AMT. What you're doing here is finding out how much of your alternative minimum tax liability came from *timing* items: items that allow you to *delay* reporting income, as opposed to items that actually *reduce* the amount of income or tax you report. If you're lucky, your entire AMT will be available as a credit in future years. But some people find that only a small portion, or none at all, is available for use as a credit.

For purposes of this book, the most important timing item is the adjustment for exercise of an incentive stock option. This is considered a timing item because the income you report upon exercise of the option for AMT purposes is income you would otherwise report later, when you sell the stock. The fact that this adjustment is a timing item helps you to qualify for the AMT credit.

Most other items you'll get hit with under the AMT don't qualify as timing items, and therefore don't give rise to AMT credit you can claim in future years. In particular, if you encounter AMT liability solely because you had a large long-term capital gain, chances are you won't qualify for the AMT credit.

Determine how much AMT credit you can use. If you have some AMT credit available from a prior year, you have to determine how much of the credit you can use in the current year. You can only use the AMT credit in a year when you're *not* paying alternative minimum tax.

The amount of AMT credit you can use is based on the difference between your regular tax and the tax calculated under the AMT rules.

> **Example:** Suppose you have $8,000 of AMT credit available from 1999. In 2000 your regular tax is $37,000. Your tax calculated under the AMT rules is $32,000. You don't have to pay AMT because your regular tax is higher than the tax calculated under the AMT rules. Better still, you're allowed to claim $5,000 of AMT credit reducing your regular tax to $32,000. You can't use the credit to reduce your regular tax below the AMT for the year, though.

In this example, you would still have $3,000 of AMT credit you haven't used. That amount will be available in 2001. In tax lingo, it's *carried forward.*

Of course, you can't claim more than the amount of the available credit. In the example, if the AMT credit available from 1999 was $2,700, then you would use the full amount of the credit in 2000. You would reduce your regular tax to $34,300—*not* all the way to $32,000.

To calculate and report your AMT credit you need to fill out *Form 8801, Credit for Prior Year Minimum Tax—Individuals, Estates and Trusts.* If you have a hard time understanding this form you have plenty of company. It's one of the most confusing forms the IRS has ever put out.

How the AMT Credit Plays Out

How will the AMT credit play out on your tax return? The answer depends on your individual circumstances. There are a few observations that may help you know what to expect.

To begin with, in normal years most people have at least a little cushion between the tax calculated under the regular income tax rules and the tax calculated under the AMT rules. The size of that cushion depends on many factors, including the number of exemptions on your tax return and the amount of state and local tax you claim as an itemized deduction. For the sake of argument, let's say your *AMT cushion* is $2,000 in a typical year.

The existence of that cushion means you can have at least a small amount of AMT adjustments without incurring any AMT at all. For example, if you exercised an incentive stock option and the adjustment was $5,000, that wouldn't be enough of an adjustment to throw you into the alternative minimum tax, because the amount of AMT on $5,000 is less than $2,000, the amount of your cushion. A $10,000 adjustment would throw you into the AMT, but only just barely, to the tune of about $800.

It's possible to use some or all of the AMT credit from exercising ISOs without selling the ISO stock.

Example: Suppose you normally have an AMT cushion of about $2,000. In the first year you exercise enough ISOs to incur $3,000 of alternative minimum tax, and this entire amount is eligible for the AMT credit. In the following year you don't have any AMT adjustments: you didn't sell your

ISO stock, and you didn't exercise any more ISOs
either. In other words, this is a "normal" year for
you. In that case, you should be able to claim
about $2,000 of your AMT credit, because of your
AMT cushion. You would have another $1,000 of
AMT credit you didn't use, and that would carry
forward to the next year.

Selling some or all of the ISO stock would help things
along. That would produce a *favorable* AMT adjustment,
as explained in Chapter 33, and increase the size of your
AMT cushion. If we change the example above so that you
sell enough ISO stock in the second year to create a
favorable adjustment of $4,000, the AMT cushion would
grow to more than $3,000 and you would be able to use
the entire credit that year.

Larger dollar amounts. Some people have incentive
stock options worth hundreds of thousands, or even
millions of dollars. If you're one of those lucky people,
you can expect to have a very large AMT liability in the
year you exercise your options—and a very large AMT
credit. A measly $2,000 AMT cushion won't take you very
far in the direction of using up the credit, so you probably
won't get much use of your credit until you sell your ISO
stock—an event that will generate a large AMT adjustment in your favor.

You may find that you can't use the entire credit even
when you've sold all of your ISO stock, however. It might
seem like you should be able to do so, but there's no rule
saying you can. The problem arises because of a mis-
match in the tax rates. When you exercise your incentive
stock options, you incur AMT liability at the rate of 28%.
The favorable adjustment permits you to reduce your
AMT in a year when you have long-term capital gain from
selling the stock. The tax rate for long-term capital gain
under the regular tax is 20%.

Example: You exercise ISOs when the spread is
$1,000,000. Your AMT liability from this transac-
tion is about $280,000. The next year, after you

satisfied the special holding period for ISO stock, you sell the stock for the same price you paid when you exercised the option. For regular tax purposes you report a long-term capital gain of $1,000,000 and pay $200,000 on that gain. The favorable AMT adjustment you receive in the year you sell the stock may allow you to claim only about $200,000 of the credit, leaving $80,000 unused.

The remaining credit will carry forward to future years. Perhaps you'll be able to use it in dribs and drabs over a number of years. When the dollar amounts are large enough, though, it's possible that you'll never recover the full value of the credit.

Part VIII
Vesting

When you receive stock in connection with services you perform, as a stock grant or as a purchase under an option or otherwise, the tax consequences depend on whether the stock was *vested* when you received it. As a general rule, if the stock is subject to a *substantial risk of forfeiture* when you receive it, you won't report income until the risk of forfeiture no longer exists.

Chapter 35 introduces terminology and explains the general rules for vesting. Chapter 36 answers frequently asked questions about how restrictions imposed by securities laws, and similar rules, affect vesting. Chapter 37 provides details on the Section 83b election, which can change the tax consequences when you receive stock that isn't vested.

Part VIII
Vesting

Chapter 35
General Rules for Vesting

It's unfortunate, but one of the most important issues relating to equity compensation is a somewhat technical one that uses arcane terminology. The basic idea here is fairly simple, though. If the company puts certain kinds of restrictions on your right to keep the stock, you don't have full ownership of it yet. That means you don't report income from receiving the stock until the restrictions go away.

Terminology

Here are some words you need to know in working with the vesting rules:

Substantial risk of forfeiture. Only certain types of restrictions will delay the reporting of income. In tax lingo, these are restrictions that create a *substantial risk of forfeiture*.

Vested. If your stock is subject to a substantial risk of forfeiture *and* is not transferable, we say it isn't *vested*. So these are two ways of saying the same thing: if it isn't vested, you have a substantial risk of forfeiture. If you don't have a substantial risk of forfeiture (or the stock is transferable), your stock is vested.

Lapse and nonlapse restrictions. The regulations distinguish between two kinds of restrictions, and give them different tax treatment. Your stock is subject to a *nonlapse restriction* if three things are true:

- The restriction requires you to sell (or offer to sell) your property under a formula price. For example, it may require you to sell for book value, or a multiple of sales or profits.

- The restriction will never go away.

- If you sell or otherwise transfer the stock to someone else, the restriction will apply to that person as well.

Any restriction that doesn't meet the requirements described above is a *lapse restriction*. Notice that a restriction can be permanent and still be a lapse restriction under this definition. Permanency is only one of the requirements for a nonlapse restriction.

Substantial Risk of Forfeiture

There's much confusion about what constitutes a *substantial risk of forfeiture*. Only certain types of risks count here. You may receive stock under circumstances where there's a very real risk that you won't ever get to sell the stock at its current value. Nevertheless, if the risk isn't a substantial risk of forfeiture, you still have to report compensation income *now*. You can't wait until the risk goes away.

Generally, you have a risk of forfeiture under these rules when your right to continue owning the stock depends on whether you continue to work for the company. The most common situation by far is where the company says you'll forfeit the stock (or have to sell it back for less than full value) if your employment terminates before a specified amount of time has elapsed.

A risk of forfeiture doesn't have to relate to a specific time period. For example, it might say you'll have permanent ownership of the stock when sales for your division reach a certain level. You can also have a risk of forfeiture based on an agreement not to compete. Perhaps you received stock in connection with termination of your employment, subject to forfeiture if you work for a competitor of the company within the next two years.

Bear in mind that the risk of forfeiture has to be *substantial*. If it's obvious that the condition for permanent ownership of the stock will be satisfied, the condition doesn't create a substantial risk of forfeiture. Same thing if there's good reason to believe the company won't enforce the forfeiture provision (for example, you control the company). An agreement not to compete may not create a substantial risk of forfeiture if you've reached retirement age or for some other reason have no real ability to compete.

Risk of Decline in Value

A risk that the stock will decline in value is *not* a substantial risk of forfeiture. This is a hard fact for many people to accept, especially if they're unable to sell the stock. You may have a situation where you can't sell the stock for a period of time, and you believe there's a risk the value of the company will decline before you can make a sale. With limited exceptions described in Chapter 36 on restrictions under the securities laws, you don't have a substantial risk of forfeiture in these circumstances. You have to report the current value of the stock as compensation income.

Rules For Vesting

The rules for vesting depend on whether you make the section 83b election. The description here assumes you did *not* make this election. Chapter 37 provides details concerning the section 83b election.

General. The tax law treats you as if you don't really own stock that isn't vested. You don't report income when you receive the stock. The time before the stock vested doesn't count for purposes of determining whether you have long-term capital gain or loss when you sell the stock. In other words, your holding period begins when the stock vests, not when you received the stock. What's more, if the stock pays dividends, you report compensation income, not dividend income, for any dividends you receive before the stock vests.

Forfeitures. If you fail to satisfy the conditions that create the risk of forfeiture, you forfeit the stock. No doubt you will consider that an economic loss. The stock was yours, and had value, and now it isn't yours any more. As a general rule, though, you can't claim a loss on your tax return. The tax law treats you as if you don't own the stock, and you can't claim a loss for something you don't own.

There's an exception to this rule. If you paid something for the stock, and didn't get that amount back at the time of the forfeiture (or got only part of it back) you can report a loss. This would be an unusual situation, because most companies won't ask you to forfeit the money you came up with to acquire the stock.

Vesting. If things go well, you'll satisfy the conditions to have unrestricted ownership of the stock. At that point the stock is *vested*. You report compensation income at that time, regardless of whether you sell the stock. The amount of income is the value of the stock at the time it vested, reduced by the amount (if any) you paid for the stock.

From that point on, you're treated as if you bought the stock on the date it vested. Even though you may have held the stock for years, you'll have short term gain or loss if you sell the stock a year or less after the vesting date. You have to hold the stock *more than a year after the vesting date* to be able to report long-term capital gain when you sell it.

The *amount* of gain or loss when you sell the stock depends on your *basis* for the stock. Your basis includes the amount of income you report when the stock vests. If you paid anything for the stock, that's included in your basis, too. So your basis is the amount (if any) paid for the stock, increased by the amount of income you report when the stock vests.

Chapter 36
Vesting and Securities Rules

It's possible you'll find yourself holding shares of stock you can't sell, at least for the time being, because of restrictions imposed by the securities laws. That's an awkward position to be in if you have to report income, and pay tax, when you receive your shares. You're likely to wonder if you can postpone reporting the income until the restriction lapses and you're able to sell the stock. With very limited exceptions, the answer is no.

Section 16b

One type of restriction is the *short swing profits rule* imposed by Section 16b of the Securities Exchange Act of 1934. Under this rule you may be required to give up any profits realized from a sale of stock that occurs within six months of a purchase. This rule *does* delay vesting for tax purposes, when it applies. But it doesn't apply very often.

For one thing, Section 16b applies only to certain officers, directors and major shareholders of companies required to file reports to the SEC. That's a small fraction of the people who receive equity compensation. If you're one of those people, you'll know it because the company's legal counsel will have informed you of things you must do—and things you must not.

Even if you find yourself on this short list, you may never have to deal with Section 16b in connection with your equity compensation. One reason is that under Section 16b—unlike the tax law—your holding period begins when you *receive* an option, not when you *exercise* it. If you hold an option for at least six months before you exercise it, you've already satisfied the Section 16b holding period when you receive the stock. What's more, the regulations under Section 16b were revised a few years ago to provide that most grants of equity compensation are exempt.

The bottom line is that Section 16b applies to relatively few people and, when it comes to equity compensation, applies in relatively few situations.

Pooling of Interests

Here's another rule that *does* delay vesting for tax purposes, but applies very rarely. The *pooling of interests* rule provides favorable accounting treatment for certain mergers and acquisitions if various technical requirements are satisfied. If your company is acquired by another one, the pooling of interests rule may prevent you from selling stock you received in the transaction. In that unlikely event, your stock isn't vested for tax purposes until the restriction ends.

> The pooling of interests rule has been marked for extinction, so this rarely used vesting rule is likely to become meaningless in the near future.

Rule 144

Now we turn to a rule that applies to *many* people who receive equity compensation. If you receive unregistered stock in a public corporation, you're likely to be required to sign an *investment letter* saying you're acquiring the stock for investment and not for resale. The stock certificate will be stamped with a legend indicating it can be sold only in accordance with certain requirements. This stock may be called *lettered stock*, or *Rule 144 stock*.

What's going on here? Companies have to comply with an elaborate (and expensive) registration requirement to bring stock to the market. This assures that investors have access to information that will enable them to make an informed decision on whether to buy the stock. The SEC doesn't want companies to sidestep this process by issuing shares to persons affiliated with the company when those people are going to turn around and sell the shares on the market. Rule 144 establishes rules under which affiliated individuals can receive, and eventually (but not immediately) sell, unregistered shares.

The problem here is that Rule 144 does *not* prevent your stock from being vested under the tax law. Why not? Perhaps because Rule 144 isn't an absolute prohibition on sale. You can't sell your stock on the open market, but you're permitted to arrange a private sale if you can find a buyer who will accept the stock subject to the restrictions of Rule 144.

Then again, a Rule 144 restriction doesn't impose a risk that you'll lose the stock. Your risk is that the stock will decline in value. But the tax regulations specify that a risk of decline in value isn't a substantial risk of forfeiture.

There's one case in which a Rule 144 restriction—coupled with an *additional* restriction imposed by the company—satisfied the court that stock should not be considered vested for tax purposes. I'm not inclined to rely on that case, however. It isn't clear to me that other courts, including the Tax Court, would follow this holding outside the New England states that are included in the First Circuit.

Generally, then, you can't use a Section 144 restriction to delay vesting. You also can't use it to reduce the value of the stock, even though you'll surely have to settle for a discount if you make a private sale before the end of the Rule 144 holding period. About all you can do with Rule 144 is grin and bear it.

Blackout Periods

Many companies impose *blackout periods* in which employees aren't permitted to trade in the company's stock. These periods are timed in relation to the company's quarterly reports. The securities laws don't require blackout periods, but they make good sense. They avoid the implication that employees used inside information to get the better of public investors who don't yet have access to that information. Blackout periods help assure the integrity of the market in the company's stock and can help avoid lawsuits from unhappy investors.

I'm not aware of any ruling that indicates whether such company-imposed restrictions prevent stock from being vested for tax purposes. There can be little doubt of the IRS view, however. The regulations state that property is vested for tax purposes when it is *either* transferable *or* not subject to a substantial risk of forfeiture. It seems reasonably clear that a restriction on transferability, by itself, will not prevent vesting. You need, in addition, a substantial risk of forfeiture. As noted earlier, the regulations plainly state that the risk of property declining in value is *not* a substantial risk of forfeiture. Conclusion: blackout periods don't delay vesting.

Lockup Periods

A similar issue arises as to *lockup periods*. These are periods in which some or all of the existing shareholders are not permitted to sell shares after a company goes public. The securities laws don't impose this requirement; a lockup is imposed by underwriters to make it easier to sell shares that are being offered to the public. As in the case of blackout periods, there is no direct authority on the issue, but my conclusion is that lockups (without some other restriction) don't delay vesting.

Perspective

I hear a lot of frustration from people who feel they shouldn't have to report income from their stock until such time as they're free to sell it on the open market. I sympathize with that feeling. At the same time, I'm aware that there are plenty of people out there who receive stock in companies that aren't publicly traded. Some of these people have no reasonable prospect of selling their stock in the near future, yet they have to report income equal to the value of the stock when they receive it. My point: the tax applies because you received something of value, *not* because you received something you can immediately sell. If you have to pay tax on receiving property you can't sell, you're in an uncomfortable position—but not a unique one.

Chapter 37
Section 83b Election

The tax rules for stock that isn't vested provide both an advantage and a disadvantage when compared to the rules for vested stock. You get the advantage of waiting until the restriction lapses before you report income. If the stock goes up in value while you're waiting, though, you'll report *more* income. A large increase in the value of your stock prior to vesting can have painful tax consequences.

If you don't like the trade-off, you can change the rules. To do this, you file the section 83b election. When you do, you'll be treated (mostly) as if you received vested stock. But you have to act fast: *the election must be made within 30 days after you receive the stock.*

Availability

The election is available when you receive stock with delayed vesting. The point of the election is to treat the stock as if it's already vested, so there's no need to file it if you receive stock that's immediately vested. You might have a situation where it isn't clear whether the stock is vested. In this case you might want to file the election just to eliminate any doubt.

The election is *not* available for *options.* With very limited exceptions, options don't produce current compensation income even if they're vested. Filing a section 83b election when you receive an option doesn't cause you to report current income and, more importantly, doesn't eliminate compensation income when you exercise the option. The election simply doesn't apply to options.

It may apply when you exercise an option, however. Some options impose restrictions so that the stock isn't vested right away when you receive it. In this case it may make sense to file the section 83b election when you exercise the option.

Effect of the Election

If you make the section 83b election, you report compensation income when you receive the stock, not when it vests. The value of the stock is determined when you receive it. You have nothing to report at the time the stock vests.

> **Example:** In return for services, you receive 4,000 shares of stock in a startup company. When you receive the stock it isn't vested, and the value is $1.25 per share. Shortly thereafter the company goes public and is hugely successful. When the shares vest two years later they're trading at $50.
>
> Without the section 83b election, you'll report nothing when you receive the shares. When the stock vests, it's worth $200,000 and you'll report that much compensation income. You may pay up to $80,000 in federal income tax as a result.
>
> The result is very different if you file the section 83b election. You would report $5,000 of compensation income when you receive the stock. You have nothing to report when the stock vests. You can continue to hold it without paying another dime of tax. If you sell the stock for $200,000, you'll have a long-term capital gain of $195,000. The tax rate will be 20%, and your total tax may be not much more than half of the amount you would have paid without the election.

Each Rose Has Its Thorns

The section 83b election doesn't always work out this well. If the stock doesn't rise in value after you make the election, you've *accelerated* tax (paid it sooner) without receiving any benefit. If the stock goes down, you've paid *more* tax than would have been necessary.

Worse, you might forfeit the stock after making the election. In this case you would deduct any amount you actually paid for the stock (subject to capital loss limitation) but you would get no deduction relative to the compensation income you reported when you made the election. That's a miserable result: the election caused you to pay tax on income you didn't get to keep, with no offsetting tax benefit later on.

When the Election Makes Sense

The section 83b election makes sense in the following situations:

- The amount of income you'll report when you make the election is small and the potential growth in value of the stock is great.

- You expect reasonable growth in the value of the stock and the likelihood of a forfeiture is very small.

Conversely, you should avoid the section 83b election where a forfeiture seems likely, or where you'll pay a great deal of tax at the time of the election with only modest prospects for growth in the value of the stock.

Don't miss this chance. You might have to accept a risk of forfeiture on your stock even though you paid full value when you received it. The way this usually works is you agree to sell the stock back for the amount you paid if you quit within a specified period. This is a risk of forfeiture even though you won't lose your original investment. The risk is that you'll lose part of the value of the stock if your employment terminates before the stock vests. *That means that if the stock goes up in value, you'll report compensation income when the stock vests.*

You can avoid this result by making the section 83b election when you buy the stock. In this situation *the election is free.* The election costs nothing because the amount of income you report is the value of the stock minus the amount you paid. You paid full value, so the amount of income is zero. Failure to make this free election can be a costly mistake.

Preparing the Election

There's no special form to use in making the election. You simply put the appropriate information on a piece of paper and send signed copies to the right people. The paper should say "Section 83b Election" at the top and begin with the words, "The taxpayer hereby elects under Section 83b as follows." Then provide the following information:

- Your name, address and social security number.

- A description of the property (for example, "80 shares common stock of XYZ corporation").

- The date you received the property and the taxable year for which you're making the election. (Unless you're one of the lonely few who have a fiscal year, you're making the election for the calendar year in which you received the stock.)

- The nature of the restriction(s) on the stock (for example, "forfeit if employment terminates before July 31, 2001").

- The fair market value at the time you received the stock. Note that for this purpose you can't use the possibility of a forfeiture or any other non-permanent restriction to reduce the value.

- The amount, if any, you paid for the stock.

- A statement as follows: "I have provided copies of this statement as required in the regulation." See below for the copies you have to provide.

Filing the Election

The key point about filing the election has already been mentioned. At risk of repeating myself: *the election has to be filed within 30 days after you receive the property.* If you don't act within that time you're out of luck. You can't wait until you file your return. Here's what you need to do:

- Within 30 days after you receive the stock, send the election to the IRS office where you file your income tax return. (Check the instructions for Form 1040 if you're not sure of the address.) *I highly recommend sending this election by certified mail and getting a stamped receipt with a legible date.*

- Provide a copy of the election to the company that granted the stock.

- In the unusual situation where you had the company transfer the stock to someone other than yourself (such as a trustee), you need to provide a copy to that person as well.

- Attach a copy of the election when you file your income tax return for that year.

This is one of those situations where it's very important to keep good records. Make sure you maintain a copy of the election, and evidence that you filed it within the time limit. The value of the stock—and the importance of this election—could grow substantially during the time it takes for the stock to vest.

Part IX
Employee Stock Purchase Plans

Employee stock purchase plans provide a tax-favored way for employees to build an investment stake in their company. These plans are *broad-based*, covering most categories of employees. They often offer a discount of up to 15% of the value of the stock, with the tax consequences of the discount deferred until you sell the stock.

Part IX
Employee Stock Purchase Plans

Chapter 38
Overview of Employee Stock Purchase Plans

Let's make sure we're on the same page. An employee stock purchase plan ("ESPP") is *not* the same as an employee stock ownership plan ("ESOP"). An ESOP is a retirement plan that invests in stock of the employer. This book doesn't cover retirement plans, so we won't be discussing ESOPs.

An employee stock purchase plan is also not an incentive stock option plan. An ISO plan issues incentive stock options. Part V of this book describes the treatment of ISOs. An employee stock purchase plan may issue options, although more often the plan works as a way for you to sign up to buy stock through payroll deduction. There are some similarities between ISO plans and employee stock purchase plans, but the tax treatment isn't the same and it's important to be clear on which is which.

> Employee stock purchase plans are sometimes called *Section 423 plans.*

Which is which? You should be able to tell which you have by looking at the materials the company provided for the plan. If you don't have those materials, request them from the appropriate office of your company. These materials are important to have in any event.

There are also a couple of tip-offs that you're looking at an ESPP. One is a discount on your purchase. An employee stock purchase plan isn't required to provide a discount, but it *may* provide a discount, and many of them do. An incentive stock option may give you a bargain price if the stock goes up while you hold the option, but you can't get an up-front discount with an ISO. The other tip-off is that the company doesn't have to make ISOs available to all employees. It can give them just to top executives, or to a select group of key people. An employee stock purchase plan can exclude certain people, such as employees who have been with the company less than two years or who generally work fewer than 20 hours per week—but otherwise has to be available to everyone.

A Good Deal

Employee stock purchase plans are a good deal for those who participate. Like incentive stock options, they make it possible for you to buy stock at a bargain price without reporting income until you sell the stock. Yet in some ways employee stock purchase plans are even better than ISOs.

One advantage is that your employee stock purchase plan can provide you with a discount. The purchase price can be as much as 15% below the value of the stock at the time the price is established. Incentive stock options have to be issued with an exercise price at or above the current value of the stock.

The other advantage—and this is a big one—is that you don't have to deal with alternative minimum tax when you buy shares under an employee stock purchase plan. AMT is a major headache in dealing with ISOs. When you buy stock under an ESPP, the AMT doesn't apply.

There's one way an ISO is better, though. Incentive stock options give you the possibility of converting *all* of your profit to long-term capital gain if you hold the stock long enough. By contrast, if you receive a discount on your purchase under an ESPP, you'll have to report some of your profit as compensation when you sell the stock, no matter how long you hold it.

Typical Terms

Employee stock purchase plans are peculiar in that the way they are described in the tax law doesn't match the way most of these plans work. The tax law describes them as plans under which employees receive options. With a few tweaks here and there, an incentive stock option plan could be turned into an employee stock purchase plan.

One of those tweaks is a pretty major one, though. An ESPP has to be made available to all full-time employees on the same basis. Most companies that adopt these plans are so large that it would be difficult to administer a plan where everyone in the company receives ISO-style options. So companies have developed a different way of implementing these plans. Instead of receiving an option, you're offered an opportunity to buy stock at a favorable price through payroll deduction. You can choose to participate or not, and the IRS treats this as an option that meets the requirements for an employee stock purchase plan.

The specifics of these plans vary from one company to the next. The following is an outline of terms that might be considered typical. It's important to check the terms of your own company's plan because those terms may differ in important ways from those described below.

- If you want to participate, you have to sign up by a particular date to have from 1% to 10% of your pay withheld to purchase company stock over a particular *offering period*.

- The money will accumulate for that period of time, and then be used to buy stock at a price equal to 85% of the *lower* of the stock value at the beginning of that period or the stock value at the end of that period. That means your worst case scenario is that the stock price stays the same or goes down, and you buy for 15% below the price at the end of the period. If you're lucky, the stock price goes up, and your bargain will be bigger. For example, if the stock price is $10 at the beginning of the offering period and $15 at the end, the purchase price will be $8.50, which is less than 60% of the $15 price at the time of the purchase.

- You can back out of the purchase at any time until close to the end of the offering period. (The deadline might be ten days before the end of the offering period, for example, to give the company time to process the paperwork.) If you withdraw from the purchase, the company will refund to you the money that was withheld from your paychecks.

The company doesn't *have* to offer a 15% discount. It can offer a smaller discount or none at all. Notice that you can still come out way ahead without a discount. In the example above, you would be purchasing $15 stock at $10 because the stock price went up during the offering period. If the stock doesn't go up during the offering period and you want to back out of the purchase, you can do so. Be sure to check the plan for the withdrawal deadline. Your only downside if you participate and then withdraw is that you don't get interest on the money that was held in the plan. That's usually a small price to pay for the possibility of buying stock at a bargain price.

How valuable is that 15% discount? It turns $85 into $100, and that's a return of over 17.5%. In a typical plan you get that return in six months, so that's an *annual* return of over 35%. But you pay in gradually over the six months rather than having the full amount tied up for that period of time, so it actually works out to an investment return of more than 70%. Where else can you get a deal like that?

Chapter 39
ESPP Tax Consequences

The beauty of an employee stock purchase plan is that you have nothing at all to report when you acquire the stock. No income on your tax return, and no alternative minimum tax either. When it comes to tax treatment of a valuable benefit from your employer, that's as good as it gets.

> I suppose it could be even better. You might want to claim a deduction for the amount of your paycheck that's used to buy the stock. Sorry, but that's not possible. You have to pay tax on that amount, just as if you received it in your paycheck and then used it to buy stock.

When it comes to selling the stock, the tax rules get a little trickier. You're still nowhere near the complexity you have to deal with under the incentive stock option rules, with dual basis and the AMT credit to worry about. But you have to work through some quirky little rules to find out how much of your profit will be treated as compensation income.

Special Holding Period

Just like ISOs, employee stock purchase plans have a special holding period. The tax treatment of your sale will depend on whether you satisfied this test. You meet the holding period requirement on the *later* of the following two dates:

- The date two years after the company granted the option.

- The date one year after you bought the stock.

Now we're back to talking about *options*. Under these plans you don't receive an option in the traditional sense, so when does the two-year period start to run? I have a hard time finding a clear answer in the law, but the IRS has taken the position in its private rulings that the two-year period begins on the same date the offering period begins. (Remember that the *offering period* is the time during which the company is taking deductions from your pay, and also the time during which the purchase price of the stock is determined.) The date of purchase is the last day of the offering period, even if it takes a while after that for the company to do the paperwork and provide you with the stock.

The offering period is often six months, but it can be shorter or longer. If it's no more than a year, you'll satisfy the special holding period if you hold the stock until the second anniversary of the start of the offering period. I've never seen an ESPP that had an offering period lasting more than a year, although that's at least a theoretical possibility. If you found yourself in such a plan, the special holding period would be satisfied when you held the stock for a year after the end of the offering period.

> Any compensation income you have under the rules described below should be reported as wages on your tax return. If the company didn't include this income on your W-2, simply add it to your W-2 income when you fill out your return.

Early Disposition

If you sell the stock, or otherwise dispose of it, before satisfying the special holding period, you have an early disposition (or *disqualifying* disposition). See Chapter 21 for details on what events count as a disposition. The same rules that apply to stock from incentive stock options apply to stock from employee stock purchase plans.

When you make an early disposition you have to report compensation income equal to the bargain element when you bought the stock—that is, at the end of the offering period. The *bargain element* is the difference between the value of the stock on that date and the amount you paid for it.

> **Example:** The stock price was $10 at the beginning of a six-month offering period and $11 at the end of that period. The employee stock purchase plan offers a 15% discount from the lower of those values, so you buy the stock at $8.50 per share. If you sell the stock—or give it away—before satisfying the special holding period, you'll report $2.50 per share of compensation income. That's the difference between the $11 value and the $8.50 purchase price.

You have to report this amount of compensation income even if you don't have a profit on the sale of the stock. (That's a difference from incentive stock options, by the way.) The compensation income increases your basis in the stock, and reduces your capital gain (or increases your capital loss).

> **Example:** In the example above you had to report $2.50 of compensation income. You paid $8.50 for the stock, and this $2.50 would increase your basis to $11 per share. If you sold the stock for $7, you would report a capital loss of $4 per share (in addition to reporting $2.50 of compensation income). If you used the stock to make a gift, you would still report $2.50 of income and the basis of the stock at the time of the gift would be $11 per share.

It's possible, of course, that you'll have a profit on your sale that's larger than the amount of compensation income you reported. In that situation you'll report capital gain in addition to compensation income. The capital gain will be long-term if you held the stock more than a year before the sale.

> You can hold the stock more than a year but still have an early disposition because the special holding period runs until two years have elapsed from the beginning of the offering period.

Example: Same as the previous example, except you sold for $15 per share. Your basis, after adjusting for the $2.50 of compensation income, is $11 per share, so you report $4 per share of capital gain.

Holding Period Satisfied

Now things get interesting. You may still have to report compensation income if you sell *after* satisfying the special holding period. The rule for determining *how much* compensation income to report is a little peculiar.

First, the good news. If you don't have any profit, you don't report any compensation income. That's a much better deal than when you make an early sale. As explained above, you have to report compensation income on an early sale, even if you sell at a loss.

If you sell at a profit, you have to report compensation income. The amount you report is the *lesser* of the amount of your profit or . . . or what? You're probably thinking it's the bargain element again—but it's not. Instead, it's the difference between the stock value *when the option was granted* (which means at the *beginning* of the offering period, not the *end*, when you bought the stock) and the *option price*, which for this purpose is *also* determined as of the beginning of the offering period.

Example: Let's stick with the example we've been using. The value of the stock at the beginning of the offering period is $10 per share, and you buy the stock for $8.50 per share at the end of that period when it's trading at $11. If you sell the stock at $14 after the end of the special holding period, you have to report compensation income equal to the difference between $10 and $8.50, or $1.50 per share. That's less than the $2.50 per share bargain element you would report if you sold before the end of the special holding period. You also report $4 per share of capital gain.

Another: Change the facts. At the end of the offering period the stock is down to $8 per share. The plan says you pay 85% of the *lower* of the price at the beginning of the offering period or the price at the end. That means you pay 85% of $8, or 6.80 per share. The stock's price recovers and you end up selling at $14. You still report compensation income of $1.50 per share, because the bargain element at the time of exercise doesn't matter. You would add $1.50 to your purchase price of $6.80 to come up with a basis of $8.30. Your capital gain on the sale would be $5.70.

If that gives you a headache, you're not alone. But believe me, this is a whole lot easier than dealing with the AMT, as you would if you had incentive stock options.

Pop Quiz

Feeling smart? Try this one. In the last example above, other things being equal, should you sell before or after satisfying the special holding period? Did you come up with the surprising answer? You do better if you sell early. The amount of ordinary income on an early sale is $1.20, the amount of the bargain element at the end of the offering period. Once you satisfy the special holding period, you have to measure your compensation income as of the *beginning* of the offering period, when the spread was $1.50 per share.

On our web site at **www.fairmark.com** you'll find updates to the material in this book and a message board where you can ask questions or post comments.

Part X
Other Topics

This part of the book covers topics you may need to understand when dealing with compensation in stock and options, even though they don't fit in the previous categories.

Part X
Other Topics

Chapter 40
Fair Market Value

When you report compensation income from stock or options, the amount of income will be measured by the *fair market value* of the stock. There's a classical definition of this term that many tax professionals know by heart:

Fair market value is the price at which the property would change hands between a willing buyer and a willing seller, neither being under any compulsion to buy or to sell and both having reasonable knowledge of relevant facts.

This definition takes you a good part of the way toward understanding the concept. To complete the picture we'll discuss the following topics:

- Valuing publicly traded stock

- Valuing privately held stock

- How restrictions affect value

- Discounts

Valuing Publicly Traded Stock

Stock is publicly traded if you can buy or sell it on an established securities market, or through some other system that acts as the equivalent of a securities market. In general the stock market determines the value of publicly traded stock. The usual rule is that the value on any given day is the average of the high and low selling prices on that day.

Employers sometimes use variations on this rule. If the stock is very thinly traded, it may make sense to use an average over a period of several trading days so that a single transaction won't have undue effect on the value. There isn't any regulation that permits this approach, but we don't see the IRS challenging reasonable variations unless they provide opportunities for manipulation.

It's somewhat unusual, but not impossible, for publicly traded stock to qualify for a blockage discount as explained below.

Valuing Privately Held Stock

If your stock isn't publicly traded as explained above, it's *privately held*. A full discussion of valuation for privately held stock is beyond our scope—there are entire books written on the subject. Here are some of the main points:

- **Recent transactions.** The strongest indication of the value of stock on a given date is an actual arm's length sale occurring near that date. A sale is at *arm's length* if there isn't any family or other relationship between the buyer and seller that might lead to a sale at a price different than fair market value. If you want to claim that your stock has a value of $10 per share, you'll have a hard time supporting that claim if someone recently paid $50 per share.

- **Other valuation methods.** Sometimes there are no recent sales that can be used to establish the value of stock. Then you have to estimate the value of the entire company and divide by the number of shares outstanding to find the value per share. Different types of methods are appropriate for different types of businesses. Most focus in some way on profits (or an element of revenues that should be indicative of profit potential), but the value of the company's assets may come into play also. The *book value* of a company (the value of its assets minus its liabilities, as shown on the company's financial records) is sometimes seen as a *minimum* value the company must have, but some companies have a value that far exceeds book value. Inevitably there's an element of subjectivity in determining the fair market value of a closely held business. As a result, taxpayers frequently find themselves in court with the IRS over valuation issues.

Effect of Restrictions

You may feel that restrictions on the stock you acquired make it less valuable than it would otherwise be. But there's a special rule here: when you determine the value of your shares, you have to ignore all restrictions except those that are permanent. If your stock is restricted for a limited period of time, or until some event occurs, you have to ignore the restriction when you determine the value of the stock.

Certain permanent restrictions count in determining value, however. The tax law refers to these as *non-lapse restrictions*. If your stock is subject to a permanent restriction, you may be able to take that restriction into account in determining the value of the stock. See Chapter 35 for details.

Discounts

There are circumstances that can justify a discount in the value of your stock. One recognized discount applies when there's no market for the stock: a discount for *lack of marketability*. Another discount can apply where there's a market for the stock, but the size of your holdings is large enough to make efficient sale impossible: a *blockage* discount. The availability of these discounts, and the appropriate size of the discount, should be determined by a qualified appraiser or tax professional.

Chapter 41
Compensation Income

Throughout this book I'll refer often to *compensation income*. Of course you're familiar with compensation income in general, going back to the first time you received a paycheck. There are two special considerations connected with equity compensation, though. First, withholding is required for certain forms of equity compensation provided to employees. When the compensation takes the form of stock, special arrangements are necessary to satisfy the withholding requirement. And second, if you're not an employee, you need to be aware of not only your income tax liability but also your obligations under the self-employment tax.

Withholding for Employees Only

Most types of equity compensation may be received by non-employees (such as directors or consultants) as well as employees. Withholding is required only for employees (and, in some cases, former employees). Note that if you aren't an employee you'll generally have to pay self-employment tax on any amount that's treated as compensation.

When Withholding Is Required

In general, withholding is required in situations where an employee is required to report compensation income:

- Withholding is required when you receive a grant of vested stock (or make the section 83b election for unvested stock).

- Withholding is required when your previously unvested stock vests (assuming you didn't make the section 83b election).

- Withholding is required when you exercise a nonqualified option.

There's an exception to this general rule. If you make a disqualifying disposition of stock acquired by exercising an incentive stock option, the IRS doesn't require withholding.

How to Meet the Withholding Requirement

The special problem in withholding on compensation paid in stock is that you aren't receiving any money. Naturally the IRS insists that the withholding be provided in cash. How can you provide cash withholding when you didn't receive any money?

Some companies help with this problem by providing some form of cash compensation that goes along with the stock. This may take the form of a stock appreciation right or cash bonus plan. Note, however, if the company covers your withholding, the amount they pay for that purpose is *additional* taxable income to you.

> **Example:** You receive stock valued at $20,000 and the withholding obligation is $6,600. If the company covers this withholding for you, then you have another $6,600 of compensation income (and the company has to withhold on *that*). The company would have to provide about $10,000 to cover all the bases at this rate of withholding. (This is called *grossing up* the payment.)

Most companies expect *you* to cover the withholding. That means you have to come up with the cash and pay it to the company, which in turn pays it to the IRS. You may have to withdraw that amount from savings, or perhaps even borrow to cover the payment. It may be possible to use the stock you're receiving as security for the loan.

One approach is to sell some or all of the stock that was provided as compensation, and use the sale proceeds to meet the withholding requirement. The company may agree to buy back some of the stock, or arrange for it to be sold by a broker, for example. In these cases you need to consider the tax effects of the sale as well as the receipt of the stock.

Consequences of Withholding

Regardless of how you satisfy the requirement, the income tax withholding will be a credit on your income tax return. It will reduce the amount of tax due or increase the amount of your refund.

Don't make the mistake of thinking the withholding is part of your cost for the stock. You can't include the withholding in the basis of the stock you received, even though it was an amount you had to pay to the company when you received it.

You should be aware that the amount of withholding on this compensation may or may not be enough to cover the amount of tax that will actually result. Withholding formulas don't precisely match the tax liability. It pays to do a calculation of the actual amount of tax you'll owe with respect to this compensation to avoid an unpleasant surprise on April 15.

Social Security and Self-Employment Tax

Social security and self-employment tax walk hand-in-hand. The first applies to employees, and the second applies to everyone else. When you're an employee, you pay half of the social security tax through withholding, and your employer pays the other half. (The half that's paid by your employer doesn't show up on your pay stub, so many people aren't aware that the employer pays "matching dollars" for the social security tax that's withheld from their pay.) If you provide services but you're not an employee, you're *self-employed*. The tax law treats you as if you were both the employer and the employee, and that means you have to pay both halves of the tax on your net earnings from self-employment.

Whether or not you're an employee, these taxes apply only to the portion of your income that counts as compensation. Whenever this book describes an element of income as *compensation income,* you can plan on being hit with one of these taxes. (Chapter 21 describes an exception for early disposition of stock from an incentive stock option.) Any income described as *capital gain* is exempt from social security tax and self-employment tax. The same is true for other investment income, such as interest and dividends (except dividends on stock that isn't vested).

Two components of the tax. The social security tax and self-employment tax are made up of two components. One component is for hospital insurance (HI), and the other covers all other programs under social security: old age, survivors and disability insurance (OASDI). There's an income limit on the OASDI portion, known as the *wage base.* There's no income limit on the HI portion. If you earn enough income as an employee to exceed the wage base, you'll have the pleasant experience of seeing your paycheck suddenly become larger at the point in the year when OASDI withholding drops out. You'll continue paying the lower HI rate, however.

The wage base is the same for both social security and self-employment tax. It's adjusted each year for inflation. For 2000 the amount is $76,200. Up to that amount, an employee pays social security tax at the rate of 7.65%, which consists of a 6.2% OASDI tax and 1.45% HI tax. Above that amount, only the 1.45% HI tax applies. All along the way, the employer is paying the same amount, too. If you're self-employed, your self-employment tax is basically double that amount, at an overall rate of 15.3% up to the wage base and 2.9% above that amount. There's a technical adjustment in these rates to give you the benefit of the deduction you would receive on the employer portion of the tax if you were actually paying wages to an employee, instead of "employing" yourself.

Finally, there are some people who have wages as an employee and also have self-employment income in the same year. In this situation, you'll get a break on the self-employment tax if your total compensation income is above the wage base. You'll pay the higher rate only on the portion of the wage base that wasn't taken up by your earnings as an employee.

Example: In 2000, you earn $60,000 as an employee and also have $30,000 of net earnings from self-employment. All of the $60,000, and the first $16,200 of self-employment earnings, will be subject to the higher rate that includes OASDI. The remaining portion of the self-employment earnings will be subject only to the lower HI tax, because it's above the $76,200 wage base.

Chapter 42
Estimated Tax Payments

If you're an employee, you may have never had to worry about making estimated tax payments. The amount of income tax withheld from paychecks may be enough to cover the tax you owe and then some, providing a refund. Even if you owe some tax on April 15, estimates aren't required unless you owe more than $1,000.

When you receive compensation in stock and options, there's a good chance you'll end up with a tax bill of more than $1,000 in one or more years. In that situation, it's possible that you'll incur a penalty if you don't make quarterly payments of estimated tax.

First Things You Should Know

If you've never had to deal with estimated taxes before, the whole idea can seem foreign and uncomfortable. There are two things you should know right away to put your mind at rest.

- **It's easy.** In most cases, the process of figuring out how much to pay isn't hard at all. And paying the tax is a snap.

- **No jail time.** You won't go to jail if you make a mistake and pay too little. In fact, the penalty isn't exactly a killer. It's just simple interest on the amount you underpaid, and the interest rate isn't terribly high. If you somehow blow it and under-pay by $400, and correct the underpayment with your next payment three months later, your penalty will be about $10. It's better to avoid the penalty, but really, this is nothing to lose sleep over.

General Rule: 90%

The general rule is that your estimated tax payments, when added to your withholding and credits, must add up to 90% of the current year's tax liability. If your withholding and credits already add up to 90% of your tax liability, you don't have to make estimated tax payments. Yet in many cases you don't have to make estimated tax payments even if your withholding and credits fall short of the 90% figure, for reasons describe below.

> When we talk about the *tax due,* we mean the total amount of tax you owe—including any self-employment tax and the dreaded alternative minimum tax (AMT).

Tax Due Less Than $1,000

Here's a rule that makes it easy for many people who have withholding that falls just a bit short to avoid dealing with estimated tax payments. No payment is required if the amount due after subtracting withholding and credits will be less than $1,000. (The amount used to be $500, but Congress increased it to $1,000 beginning in 1998.)

Example: Suppose you expect your wage withholding to be just enough to cover your income tax liability. Then you have a $4,000 long-term capital gain you didn't plan on. This gain will be taxed at 20%, so the added tax is $800. You can make an estimated tax payment if you feel more comfortable doing so, but there won't be a penalty if you wait until April 15 of next year to send in the payment because it's less than $1,000.

The only problem with this rule is that sometimes it's difficult to know what your tax liability will be. But $1,000 is a reasonable amount of leeway for the majority of taxpayers.

Prior Year Safe Harbor

Most people can avoid paying estimated tax if their withholding and credits equal 100% of the tax shown on the *prior year's* income tax return. I call this the *prior year safe harbor.*

There's a related rule. You don't have to pay estimated tax if all of the following are true:

- You had no tax liability for the previous year.

- You were a U.S. citizen or resident for the entire year.

- Your tax year covered a 12-month period.

This rule often permits taxpayers to avoid making estimated payments if they receive a large sum of income on a one-time basis.

> **Example:** In a normal year withholding is enough to cover your income tax—in fact, you usually get a small refund. In 2000 you exercise an incentive stock option and then sell the stock. As a result, you report $200,000 of income. Despite this huge increase in income, you don't have to make estimated tax payments if your withholding will be at least equal to the tax shown on the prior year's tax return.

> **Higher income, higher percentage.** There's a rule that requires taxpayers with adjusted gross income above $150,000 on the prior year's return ($75,000 if married filing separately) to use a higher percentage of the prior year's tax when applying the prior year safe harbor. To keep you on your toes, Congress changes the percentage almost every year. For 1999, people in this category had to cover 105% of their 1998 tax. Late in 1999, they decided the percentage for 2000 would be 108.6% of the 1999 tax. Go figure.

Even if the prior year safe harbor doesn't allow you to completely avoid making estimated tax payments, it permits you to determine an amount that will avoid a penalty without making an accurate estimate of the current year's taxes.

> **Example:** Your income tax for 1999 was $24,000. You expect your withholding for 2000 to be $21,000. You don't know how much income you'll have for 2000, though, because you may sell stock at a gain. Because of the prior year safe harbor, you can safely cover your estimated tax requirement by paying $3,000 ($750 per quarter). When added to your $21,000 of withholding, you'll have total payments that equal your prior year's tax.

There are situations where it doesn't make sense to use the prior year safe harbor. You may have a year in which you had an unusually large amount of income. When the next year rolls around, you would be paying estimates that are larger than necessary if you pay based on that banner year. In this case you'll want to estimate the current year's tax and try to pay at least 90% of that number.

> **Example:** In 2000 you exercised nonqualified options and reported an extra $80,000 of income. In 2001 you won't have that extra income, but still need to make estimated tax payments. If you base

the payment amount on your 2000 tax, you'll pay $30,000 more than necessary. It makes more sense to use a realistic estimate of your 2001 tax.

Estimating Your Tax

As you've seen above, there are plenty of situations where it isn't actually necessary to do any estimating when you make estimated tax payments. But sometimes you need to make an estimate of the current year's tax. Otherwise you'll either pay way too much, or come up short and end up with a penalty.

Form 1040-ES (the form used to pay estimated tax) comes with a worksheet you can use to estimate how much tax you'll owe for the current year. There's certainly nothing wrong with using this worksheet—but most people don't. The reason is that the worksheet takes you through more detail than may be necessary, but still leaves you with nothing better than an educated guess about your tax liability. You don't file the worksheet with the IRS, and there's no requirement to justify how you came up with the amount of your estimated tax payment. So most people use a somewhat simplified method to figure their estimated tax:

- Look at each number on the prior year's tax return and ask yourself if this year's number is likely to be significantly different. Ignore differences in wages because there will be a corresponding difference in withholding. Use rounded numbers and don't worry about minor changes.

- Add up all the differences to see how much larger or smaller your taxable income will be for the current year.

- Apply the tax rates to see how much difference this will make in your income tax. (If the difference results from a long-term capital gain, apply the capital gain tax rates.) Round the number up or simply tack on an added amount if you want to increase your comfort level about avoiding a penalty.

Many people using this method don't bother looking up the changes in the tax rates that result from inflation adjustments. These changes will decrease your tax slightly, so that's one way of providing a cushion of extra payments.

Voluntary Payments

Depending on your situation, the amount of estimated tax you're *required* to pay could be quite a bit less than your true estimate of the amount of tax you'll owe. That's because you're allowed to pay estimates based on the previous year's tax, even if you know this year's tax will be higher. When that happens you have a choice. You can pay the minimum amount required—and pay the rest on April 15. Or you can pay something close to the true estimate so you won't owe a lot on April 15. Which is better depends on your comfort level and money management skills.

Pay now and relax. Some people choose to make estimated payments even when the payments aren't required. The reason? Perhaps they're concerned that the money won't be there when they need it to pay taxes. Perhaps they're simply more comfortable knowing that they won't have a huge tax bill in April. There are a variety of good reasons to make estimated tax payments even if the payments aren't legally required. The biggest one is peace of mind.

Pay later and earn. The main reason *not* to pay more than you have to is that you lose the use of your money between the time you pay the estimate and the time you would have sent payment with your return. You should be able to earn at least a little bit of interest during that time. So there's at least one good reason to pay later, even though there are good reasons to pay sooner.

Which is better. Which approach is better—making voluntary payments, or paying the minimum—depends on your personality and your circumstances. Consider the following example:

Example: You normally don't pay estimates because almost all of your income is from wages subject to withholding. In January, 2000 you sell stock and have a capital gain of $30,000. You expect to owe $6,000 of tax, but you don't have to pay estimates because your 2000 withholding will be at least equal to your 1999 tax.

You have several choices, including the following:

- You can put $6,000 aside in an interest bearing account until April 15, 2001 when the tax is due. This way you can make a little profit on the money before sending it to the IRS. If you have the discipline to leave the money alone, you come out ahead using this approach. There's a danger, though. If you start with this intention, but end up spending the money on a trip to Aruba, or losing it when you try to cash in on a dot com IPO, you may wake up with a headache on April 15, 2001.

- You can send in a single estimated payment of $6,000. This approach is easy, and may seem relatively painless if you do it at a time when you're flush with money from the stock sale. It's also very safe: this approach assures that you won't somehow lose or spend the money before you file your tax return. It doesn't allow you to earn interest on the $6,000, though.

- You can send in four quarterly estimates of $1,500 each. You may prefer this approach if you don't like the idea of writing a single check for $6,000 to the IRS (who does?). And this approach gives you the flexibility to reduce later payments if you have a capital loss or other reduction in taxable income later in the year. There's a little more paperwork involved in this approach though, and more opportunity to lose or spend the money before you file your return.

There's nothing illegal or immoral about any of these approaches. They're all equally acceptable to the IRS. (They won't be upset if they receive a $6,000 payment for one quarter and no payment in later quarters.) If you find yourself in a situation like this, choose the approach that works best for you.

Increasing Your Withholding

There's a way you may be able to cover your extra tax liability without making estimated tax payments: increase the amount of tax withheld from your paycheck. You get a special benefit with this approach: extra withholding that comes late in the year is treated the same as if it was spread evenly over the year. You can use this approach to avoid late payment penalties.

How to do it. To increase the amount of federal income tax withheld from your paycheck, ask your employer for a new Form W-4. You're required to fill out this form when you start working for an employer. You can fill out a new one whenever your circumstances call for a change in the amount of withholding.

This form contains several worksheets, and the instructions tell you to "complete all worksheets that apply." But the worksheets are there mainly to make sure you don't *reduce* your withholding more than you're supposed to. There's never a problem when you want to *increase* your withholding. You can fill out the worksheets if you want, but you're not required to do so. And there's no particular need if the only thing you're doing is increasing your withholding to cover tax on your equity compensation.

There are two ways to increase your withholding on this form. One is to reduce the number of allowances you claim on the form. This can be a little tricky, because you don't necessarily know how much your withholding will change when you change your allowances. The amount depends on your income level and the withholding method adopted by your employer.

> Some people are confused by *allowances*. You get one allowance for each exemption you can claim on your tax return (yourself, your spouse and your dependents), but an allowance isn't the same as an exemption. There are allowances for other items, such as deductions and certain credits. Reducing your allowances doesn't mean you'll claim fewer exemptions when you file your tax return. The number of allowances is used *only* to determine how much tax is withheld from your paycheck.

There's another approach that's simpler: request an "additional amount" to be withheld from your paycheck. Do this on line 6 of the form. This makes it fairly easy to determine the amount of the increase when you file Form W-4.

Check with your employer to find out when the change will go into effect. Normally there's a time lag between the day you fill out this form and the day it's processed, so you may not see the change in your very next paycheck. Keep an eye on your paycheck stubs to confirm that the change was properly made, and had the effect you anticipated.

Avoiding late payment penalty. The nice thing about using withholding to cover your estimated tax liability is that it can get you out of a late payment penalty. Withholding is presumed to be received evenly through-out the year.

Example: Suppose you realize in May that you need to pay $6,000 estimated tax for the year, and you've already blown the first $1,500 payment that was due April 15. It won't be a big deal if you send in the payment a few weeks late because the penalty isn't all that terrible. But you can avoid the penalty altogether by increasing your withholding for the rest of the year by $6,000. The IRS will assume the withholding occurred evenly throughout the year, with $1,500 coming in the first quarter. You get the benefit of this assumption even if all of the added withholding comes in December!

Making Estimated Payments

Estimated payments for any year are due on April 15, June 15 and September 15 of that year, and January 15 of the following year. Whenever one of these dates falls on a legal holiday or on a weekend, the due date is the next day that isn't a holiday or weekend day. Here are some points to keep in mind:

- If you owe money with your tax return, *and* have to make an estimated tax payment, you have *two* checks to write on April 15. Be prepared!

- Although the payments are "quarterly," they aren't three months apart. The second payment sneaks up on you, just two months after the first one.

- Like your tax return, estimated payments are considered "on time" if you *mail* them by the due date.

- Most states that have an income tax require estimated payments on the same schedule as the federal payments. If you itemize deductions, it may be to your advantage to make your fourth quarter state estimated tax payment in December, not January, so you can deduct it a year earlier.

- A small number of individual taxpayers use a fiscal tax year that ends with a month other than December. Their payment schedule is different (but equivalent): the fifteenth day of the fourth, sixth and ninth months of their fiscal year, and the fifteenth day of the first month of the following fiscal year.

What to file. When you make estimated tax payments you need to enclose Form 1040-ES, Estimated Tax Voucher. This form is about as simple as they get. It asks for your name, address and social security number—and just one other item: the amount you're paying.

If you've previously made estimated tax payments, the IRS will send forms with your name, address and social security number pre-printed. Even if this is your first year paying estimates, the IRS will send pre-printed forms after they receive your first payment. You're not *required* to use these forms—don't panic if you lose them—but the IRS *prefers* that you use them to help assure that your payment will be processed promptly and correctly.

Form 1040-ES comes from the IRS as part of an intimidating package that includes lengthy instructions and detailed worksheets. As mentioned earlier, you don't have to fill out the worksheets unless you think they'll be helpful. And you should *never* send these worksheets to the IRS.

Other important tips. *Estimated tax payments don't go to the same address as your return!* Don't enclose an estimated tax payment with your Form 1040. Check the instructions for Form 1040-ES for the proper address.

Enclose your check. Write your social security number on the check and a notation of what it's for, like this: 2000 2Q Form 1040-ES. If you're doing this before your first cup of coffee in the morning, double check to see that you *signed* the check.

You don't have to justify your estimated tax payments. In fact, there's no place for a *signature* on the form. When you send it in, you're not promising that this is the correct amount. All you're saying is, "Here's a payment on account."

Be sure to keep an accurate record of your estimated tax payments so you can claim credit for them when you file your return.

Joint payments. If you're married, you can make joint estimated tax payments with your spouse. (There's an exception if either spouse is a nonresident alien.) Paying joint estimated payments does *not* mean you have to file a joint return. But if you end up filing separately, you'll have to sort out who gets credit for what amount.

Chapter 43
Identifying Shares

If you find yourself holding different batches of shares in the same company, you may want to be able to choose which shares you sell first. That's especially true when dealing with equity compensation. Selling the wrong shares can be disastrous.

Example: You hold some shares of stock you bought on the open market, and also some shares of stock from exercising an incentive stock option. You intend to sell the shares you bought on the open market. If you make a mistake and sell the shares from the incentive stock option, you may have a disqualifying disposition and be required to report compensation income.

The rules for identifying shares aren't difficult, but are often misunderstood. Many brokers are confused by them. Make sure *you* understand them, so your broker's ignorance won't cost you tax dollars.

Background

It's useful to understand the *theory* of the rule before you understand the rule. The tax law permits you to decide what shares you want to sell. But you have to make that choice *at the time of the sale*. You can't go back later, after you see how things turn out for the year, and say you really meant to sell different shares. The rules for identifying shares are designed to do two things:

- Provide a rule for what happens if you didn't make any choice at the time of the sale, and

- Provide a way for you to make a choice at that time—and to prove that you made it.

If You Don't Choose

If you don't specify which shares you're selling, the law treats you as if you sold the *earliest* shares you bought. This is called the *first-in, first out* method, or *FIFO*.

> **Example:** You bought 50 shares of XYZ at $40 in 1995 and another 50 at $60 in 1996. In 2000 you sell 50 shares at $80 without specifying which shares you're selling. The tax law says you sold the shares you bought in 1995.

Notice that you would report a smaller gain, and pay less tax, if you specified that you were selling the shares you bought in 1996. Sometimes it pays to choose which shares you're selling.

> **No averaging.** Some people wonder if they can use the *average* basis for the shares they hold. There are averaging rules for mutual fund shares, but for regular stocks you can't use average basis.

> **Switching permitted.** Suppose you sold some shares earlier and didn't identify the shares you were selling. Does this mean you're locked into using the first-in, first-out method? Not at all. The rule for identifying stock applies to each individual sale. You can identify shares for a current sale even if you failed to identify shares from the same stock in the past. (Note, however, that if you elect averaging for mutual fund shares you're locked into that method for all shares of the same mutual fund.)

If You Hold Certificates

Shares of stock are represented by *certificates*. It used to be commonplace (and is still not unusual) for shareholders to hold certificates for their shares. Most investors nowadays leave the certificates with the broker.

If you hold certificates for your shares, the way you choose which shares you're selling is to deliver the certificate that represents those shares. It isn't necessary to *identify* the shares in this situation. It's your responsibility to determine which certificate represents the shares you want to sell and deliver that certificate. It won't help to tell the broker (or the IRS) you meant to sell some other shares if you deliver the wrong certificate.

It's possible you'll end up holding a single certificate that represents shares bought at different times or different prices. In that case, assuming you're using a broker to sell the shares, you need to identify the shares you're selling (as explained below) when you deliver the certificate to the broker. If you sell some of the stock represented by a certificate *without* using a broker or other agent, you simply have to maintain a written record of which shares you sold.

How to Identify Shares

Now we come to the meat of the question. You left your shares with your broker and you want to sell some but not all of them. To identify the shares you're selling you need to do two things:

- *At the time of the sale,* specify to the broker the shares you're selling, *and*

- *Within a reasonable time thereafter,* receive a written confirmation of that specification from your broker.

Clearing the Air

Before we go another step let's clear up the biggest point of confusion. The traditional way to specify the shares you're selling is in the form of an instruction to your broker:

Sell 50 shares XYZ from the lot purchased on March 12, 1996.

This makes it sound like the broker has to do something special—possibly locate those specific shares, or at least make a record of some kind indicating what shares you sold. Some brokers say, "We don't offer that service." But in reality the only thing the broker has to do, besides executing the sale transaction in the normal way, is send you a written confirmation that you specified shares from the lot purchased on March 12, 1996.

Only part of the message shown above is really an instruction. "Sell 50 shares XYZ" is an instruction. The rest of the message is there for the sole purpose of establishing proof acceptable to the IRS that you made a choice at the time of the sale. *Your broker doesn't have to do anything about the second part of the message—except provide written confirmation that they received it.*

If I seem to be shouting here, it's because I've seen brokers time and again misunderstand this rule. They'll tell you it's okay to do your own identification on your tax return, or that their computers aren't set up to handle this, or some other nonsense. Don't believe them. They don't know what they're talking about. Tell them that's all very nice but you need written confirmation of your identification.

Specifying the Shares

When you specify the shares to be sold, you need to identify the shares in a way that makes it clear which shares you sold. Any of the following might do the trick:

- The shares I bought on March 12, 1996.

- The shares I bought for 40-3/8.

- The shares I bought most recently.

In theory, it shouldn't matter if the instruction is meaningless to the broker. For example, you may have had a different broker when you bought the shares, so the present broker has no idea what shares you bought on March 12, 1996. The thing that *does* matter is that your choice is objective and unambiguous, so you can prove to the IRS which shares you sold.

If you do your trading online, you may find that there's no apparent way to give instructions as to which shares you're selling. If you're in this situation, it should be acceptable if you send an email at the same time as your order, saying something like this:

My sale order # 123456 pertains to shares purchased on March 12, 1996. Please acknowledge in writing that you received this message at the time of the sale.

I don't guaranty that they'll respond in writing, but in my view this procedure will work if you can get them to do so. The regulations say you have to specify the shares at the time of the sale, but they don't require you to specify them as part of the process of giving the sale order.

> Be careful not to send an email that can be misinterpreted as an *additional* sale order.

Instruction need not be in writing. Although you need confirmation from the broker in writing, your *instruction* does *not* have to be in writing. It can be given by email, or orally over the telephone.

Broker's Confirmation

The second requirement is that you receive written confirmation of the identification from the broker within a reasonable time after the transaction. Remember, they're merely confirming *your message.* They don't have to confirm that they actually sold those specific shares. *All you need is written confirmation that you identified the stock at the time of the sale.*

Example: Your broker sends you a message stating "We acknowledge that you identified the 500 shares of XYZ sold on May 18, 2000 as shares purchased on March 12, 1996."

That's it! If you can extract that in writing from your broker within a reasonable time after the sale, you've met the requirement. Traditional brokers who know how to handle identification may acknowledge the identification on the trade confirmation slip, but this isn't a requirement. You just need something in writing that confirms your identification.

Email? No one knows for sure whether email confirmation is good enough because there's no guidance on this question. The regulations require a *written document* from your broker, and it's possible the IRS will say that email doesn't pass muster. You're safer if you can get your broker to send confirmation of your instructions by regular mail.

> **Note:** One taxpayer won a case where all of the communications were oral, and there was no written confirmation from his broker. I think the result of that case is questionable, so I'm reluctant to rely on it.

Blanket Instructions

Some advisors suggest that you can give your broker a blanket instruction, such as "always sell the shares with the highest basis." If you have written confirmation of such an instruction from your broker it should stand up in court. Bear in mind, though, that there may be times when you want to use a different approach. For example, it may be better to sell the shares with a lower basis because they produce long-term capital gain instead of short-term gain. You may get better results if you make a specific identification each time you sell some but not all of your shares.

Separate Accounts

The regulations don't mention the possibility of holding your shares in separate accounts. It's reasonably clear, though, that if you do so, the separate accounts serve as at least a partial identification of the shares you're selling. If you sell the shares in Account A, you don't have to specify that you aren't selling the shares in Account B, because that's already clear. It may make sense to keep your ISO shares in a separate account from any other shares you own, for example.

Chapter 44
The Wash Sale Rule

People who trade stocks often run into the wash sale rule, and you may encounter it in connection with stock you receive from your company, too. This rule prevents you from claiming a loss from a sale of stock if you buy replacement stock in the same company shortly before or after the sale.

General Rule

In general you have a wash sale if you sell stock at a loss, and buy substantially identical securities within 30 days before or after the sale.

> **Example:** On March 31 you sell 100 shares of XYZ at a loss. On April 10 you buy 100 shares of XYZ. The sale on March 31 is a wash sale.

The *wash sale period* for any sale at a loss consists of 61 days: the day of the sale, the 30 days before the sale and the 30 days after the sale. (These are calendar days, not trading days. Count carefully!) For a wash sale on March 31, the wash sale period includes all of March and April. If you want to claim your loss as a deduction, you need to avoid purchasing the same stock during the wash sale period.

Consequences of a Wash Sale

The wash sale will actually have *three* consequences:

- You aren't allowed to claim the loss on your sale.

- Your disallowed loss is added to the basis of the replacement stock.

- Your holding period for the replacement stock includes the holding period of the stock you sold.

The first one is clear enough, but the others may require some explanation.

Basis Adjustment

The basis adjustment is important: it preserves the benefit of the disallowed loss. You'll receive that benefit on a future sale of the replacement stock.

> **Example:** Some time ago you bought 80 shares of XYZ at $50. The stock has declined to $30, and you sell it to take the loss deduction. But then you see some good news on XYZ and buy it back for $32, less than 31 days after the sale
>
> You can't deduct your loss of $20 per share. But you add $20 per share to the basis of your replacement shares. Those shares have a basis of $52 per share: the $32 you paid, plus the $20 wash sale adjustment. In other words, you're treated as if you bought the shares for $52. If you end up selling them for $55, you'll only report $3 per share of gain. If you sell them for $32 (the same price you paid to buy them), you'll report a loss of $20 per share.

Because of this basis adjustment, a wash sale usually isn't a disaster. In most cases, it simply means you'll get the same tax benefit at a later time. If you receive the benefit later in the same year, the wash sale may have no effect at all on your taxes.

There are times, though, when the wash sale rule can have truly painful consequences.

- If you don't sell the replacement stock in the same year, your loss will be postponed, possibly to a year when the deduction is of far less value.

- If you die before selling the replacement stock, neither you nor your heirs will benefit from the basis adjustment.

- You can also lose the benefit of the deduction permanently if you try to get around the wash sale rule by using your IRA to buy replacement stock. There's no clear guidance on this issue, but I believe the IRS can disallow the loss permanently in this situation.

Holding Period

When you make a wash sale, your holding period for the replacement stock includes the period you held the stock you sold. This rule prevents you from converting a long-term loss into a short-term loss.

> **Example:** You've held shares of XYZ for years and it's been a dog. You sell it at a loss but then buy it back within the wash sale period. When you sell the replacement stock, your gain or loss will be long-term—no matter how soon you sell it.

In some situations you get more tax savings from a short-term loss than a long-term loss, so this rule generally works against you.

> The wash sale rule applies only to losses. You can't use the wash sale rule to avoid reporting a gain by purchasing replacement stock.

Chapter 45
Protecting Gains Without Selling

When your stock or options become very valuable, it makes sense to think about protecting your gains. The simplest way to do this may be to exercise the options and sell the stock. The tax consequences of that action may be painful, though. Are there ways you can protect your gains without incurring the tax consequences?

The answer is a qualified yes. There are some things you can do, but overall this is an extremely complicated area. It would take an entire book to provide a complete explanation of all the rules you may run into. This chapter lays out some of the main points.

Short Sales

One way to protect a built-in gain is through a *short sale*. When you sell short, some or all of the loss you have from a decline in the value of your stock or options will cancel out. This technique provides limited tax benefits, however:

- A short sale is treated as a disqualifying disposition of immature ISO stock or ESPP stock.

- A short sale prevents your stock from "aging" for purposes of getting long-term capital gain when you sell it.

- A short sale may be treated as a *constructive sale* in the year of the short sale, rather than in a later year when you dispose of your stock.

How a short sale works. A short sale is a transaction in which you sell stock that's owned by someone else. If you tell your broker to sell 100 shares of XYZ short, your broker will *borrow* 100 shares from another account and sell them. Your account gets credit for the cash, and you owe a debt: not a cash debt, but an obligation to pay back the stock you borrowed. In stock market lingo, you now have a *short position* in the stock.

A regular stock owner—someone with a *long* position—is hoping that the price of the stock will go up. When you're short, the opposite is true. If the price of the stock goes up, you'll have to pay more to buy the shares you need to repay your debt. You'll make money if the stock goes down, because then you can buy the stock cheaply and return the shares you sold earlier when the price was higher.

> **Example:** When the price of XYZ is $35 you sell 100 shares short. Your brokerage account gets credit for $3,500. Later, you satisfy your obligation to return the 100 shares of XYZ by buying them at $32. You're left with a profit of $300, less brokerage commissions.

> When you have a short position, you're in exactly the opposite stance from someone who owns the stock. You make money when the stock goes down, and lose when it goes up.

Usual tax treatment. Generally speaking, you don't report any income or gain at the time you make a short sale. Even though you received money when you made the short sale, you don't know yet whether you're going to have a gain or loss. You find that out when you close the short sale by delivering the stock you owe. The cost of the stock you use to close the short sale determines whether you have a gain or a loss on the transaction. Limitations on this tax treatment are discussed below.

Short against the box. The strange thing about selling short is that you can do it even if you already own shares in that company. For example, if you own 100 shares of

XYZ and want to sell 100, you can either sell the shares you own—or keep the shares you own and make a short sale. On Wall Street they call this going *short against the box.*

If you're short against the box, you've neutralized your market position. If the stock price goes up, the value of the shares you hold will increase, but the value of your short position will go down by the same amount. A similar cancellation occurs if the stock price goes down.

Selling short against the box would seem to be an ideal way to lock in your gains without paying tax:

> **Example:** You have 1,000 shares of your company's stock from exercising a nonqualified option. The stock price has gone sky high since you exercised the option. If you sell the stock, you'll have to report a large gain. Worse, the gain will be short term because you exercised the option less than a year ago. You're worried that the stock price may be ready to dive.
>
> Instead of selling the stock you own, you instruct your broker to make a short sale against the box. Because you've sold borrowed stock, instead of stock you own, you don't report gain or loss on the short sale. You have the cash from the sale, though, so you've locked in your gains from the stock. Later, you'll have a choice: you can close the short sale using the shares you already own, or buy new shares to close the short sale.

Limitations on Using Short Sales

In an ideal world you would be able to use a short sale in this manner to protect the gain in your stock or options indefinitely while avoiding negative tax consequences. The tax law isn't that generous, however. Here are the main limitations on using this approach:

Immature ISO and ESPP stock. A short sale against the box should not be used to protect gains in stock from an incentive stock option or employee stock purchase plan before you've satisfied the special holding period. The IRS says this is a disqualifying disposition of the stock. That means you have to report compensation income at the time you make the short sale, even if you eventually use other stock to close the short sale.

Short-term holding period. If your stock has a short-term holding period when you make the short sale, its holding period will re-start when you close the short sale. As a result, the short sale may prevent you from using long-term capital gain rates when you eventually sell your stock.

> **Example:** You've held your stock for nine months, and the price has gone up substantially in that period of time. To protect your gain, you make a short sale against the box. Six months later you buy stock in the open market to close the short sale. You still own the original stock, and you've held it more than a year. Nevertheless, any gain from this stock will be short-term unless you hold it at least a year and a day beyond the date you closed the short sale.

This rule doesn't apply if the stock was already long-term at the time you entered into the short sale. In the example above, if you held the stock at least a year and a day before you made the short sale, any gain or loss on sale of the stock would be long-term. There's a rub, here, though. If you have a loss on the short sale, you'll have to treat that as a long-term loss. That may reduce the benefit of receiving a long-term gain from this stock or from other transactions.

Constructive sales. It gets worse. At one time it was possible to be short against the box for an indefinite period of time without having to report income or gain. The law now provides that you have to report a *constructive sale* of your stock if you're short against the box for an extended period of time. The rule applies only to *appreciated financial positions*—in other words, stock or options that would produce a gain if you sold them for fair market value.

To avoid a constructive sale, you need to close the short position by January 30 of the year after you established it, and continue to hold the long position (the stock) without a protective short position for at least 60 days. Otherwise you'll be treated as if you sold the original stock on the day you entered into the short sale.

> **Example:** You hold stock that has gone up in value since you bought it. In November, you make a short sale against the box. If you continue to hold the short position at the end of the following January, you'll have to report a sale of the stock in the year you made the short sale.
>
> To avoid this, you buy stock on the open market on January 20 and use this stock to close your short position. You continue to own the original shares. You'll still have to report a sale in the previous year if you establish a new short position in the following 60 days. If you bear the market risk of holding the stock *without* an offsetting short position for at least 60 days, you avoid having to report gain in the year of your short sale.

Using Market Options

Another possible way to protect your profits without selling your stock is to use *market options*—options you buy and sell through a broker. You can hedge against the risk of loss on your stock by buying a put option, or selling a call option—or both.

A *call option* is the same type of option you receive from your employer. It provides the holder with the right to purchase stock at a specified price. A *put option* provides the holder with the right to *sell* the stock at a specified price.

> **Example:** You hold 1,000 shares of your company's stock, and they have gone up in value since you

acquired them. You buy 10 put options (each put option applies to 100 shares) to sell at the current price. If the stock's price plummets, you can exercise the put option, forcing the person who sold the option to buy the stock at the favorable price that prevailed at the time you bought the option.

If the price goes up or stays the same, you won't exercise the put option. You'll lose the cost of the put option, but you won't complain because it acted as an insurance policy against the stock going down.

Selling a call option provides protection in a different way. You don't gain direct protection against the stock going down in value because you don't have a right to force a sale. But you've received a payment for the option (called the option *premium*), and that payment will at least partially offset any loss you have from a decline in the value of the stock. When you sell a call option, you give up the benefit of a future increase in the value of your stock, because the option will be exercised if the stock price goes up.

In some situations, people do *both*. They buy a put option and sell a call option at the same time. It may be possible to select options that have matching prices: the cost of the put option is the same as the amount you receive for selling the call option. In stock market lingo, this is a *costless collar*. It didn't cost you anything to put it in place, and it puts an upper and lower limit on your profit from the stock.

Unfortunately, these techniques invoke many complicated rules, and some of the issues don't have clear answers. The rules are so technical that you may have a hard time finding a tax professional who is well versed in them. What follows is the tip of the iceberg:

Immature ISO and ESPP stock. You shouldn't be considered to have made a disqualifying disposition of your immature stock from an incentive stock option or employee stock purchase plan if you buy a put option or sell a call option, provided that the option isn't in the money at the time you do this. The contrary may be true if the option is in the money, or if you do *both* (buy a put and sell a call).

Short-term holding period. Here again you can end up with a short-term holding period even after you've held the stock more than a year. This is part of a very complicated set of rules called the *straddle rules*, and works much like the short sale rule described above.

Constructive sales. You can have a constructive sale as a result of option transactions, just as you can from a short sale against the box. You shouldn't have a constructive sale if you buy a put or sell a call when the option isn't in the money. If the option is in the money, or you use both techniques at once, you may have a constructive sale.

Loss deferral. If the combination of your stock holdings and your option position is a *straddle* under the tax rules, you can't claim a loss from one position if you have an unrecognized gain in the other position.

Generally speaking, the straddle rules are quite complicated. They include rules under which you can avoid some of the negative consequences of holding a straddle if you sell *qualified covered calls*. Details on these rules are beyond the scope of this book.

Chapter 46
Reporting Sales of Stock

When you sell stock through a broker you'll receive a form reporting the results of that sale: Form 1099-B. This form does *not* tell how much gain or loss to report. It merely tells how much you received from the sale. It's up to you to figure how much gain or loss you report from the sale, and whether the gain or loss is long-term or short-term. If you don't report your full basis in the stock, you may inadvertently pay tax on the same income twice.

Chapters describing different types of transactions (such as exercise of nonqualified options or incentive stock options) tell how to determine your *basis* and your *holding period.* You need those two pieces of information, in addition to the amount of *proceeds* from the sale, to report the sale on your return. Generally, sale proceeds are equal to the sale price of the stock minus any brokerage commissions, SEC fee and other selling expenses.

> The SEC fee is a small fraction of the selling price for shares sold in the stock markets, which is used to fund enforcement efforts of the SEC. Unless you sell a huge amount of stock, this fee will be tiny.

Schedule D

You report capital gains and losses on Schedule D, which is an attachment to Form 1040. The front of that form is in two parts, one for short-term gain or loss and one for long-term gain or loss. So the first thing you need to know is whether your holding period is a year or less (short-term) or at least a year and a day (long-term). If you sell exactly on the first anniversary of the day you acquired the stock, your gain or loss is short-term. Once you have the right part of the form, proceed as follows:

- In column (a) write a simple description of what you sold. There's an example right on the form: "100 sh XYZ Co."

- In column (b) write the date acquired. Use the date that measures your holding period, rather than the date you literally acquired the stock. For example, if the stock wasn't vested when you received it, and you didn't make the section 83b election, use the date the stock *vested* as the date acquired. If you made a single sale of shares that were acquired on more than one date, write "various" in this column. But don't combine long-term and short-term shares in a single group, even if you sold them all at once.

- In column (c) write the date of sale. For stock sold on a stock exchange, this is the *trade date*, not the settlement date.

- Column (d) on the form is labeled "sales price." If you received a Form 1099-B for the sale (as you should have if you sold your stock through a broker) you should report the same number here as appears on the Form 1099-B. Otherwise, report the proceeds from the sale minus any selling expenses.

- Column (e) is where you report your cost or other basis. Be sure to include any amount reported as compensation when you acquired the stock (or when it vested). Also, if your broker didn't subtract the brokerage commission and other selling expenses when reporting your sale proceeds on Form 1099-B, you have to add those items to your basis.

- Subtract the number in column (e) from the number in column (d), and write the result in column (f). If the number is positive, you have a capital gain. If the number is negative, indicate this by writing it in parentheses. Some software programs use a minus sign instead of parentheses and that's okay too, but easier to miss when reading a return quickly.

Follow the rest of the instructions for this form to combine your gain or loss with any other capital gains and losses, then transfer the number to the appropriate line on Form 1040.

> **Long-term gain? Caution:** Many people forget that they need to do a special rate calculation if they have a long-term capital gain. This is where you get your tax savings from the special capital gains rate, so don't make this mistake! If you're preparing the return yourself without the aid of tax software, you'll have to follow instructions carefully. It's worth the effort, because it lowers your taxes.

The IRS wants you to attach an explanation if you use something other than the actual cost of the stock as your basis. You might attach a statement that looks something like this:

> John Q. Public
> SSN 123-45-6789
> 1999 Form 1040, Schedule D
>
> The basis used for 1000 shares of XYZ stock includes $25,000 of compensation income reported in 1998 in connection with the purchase of the shares pursuant to a nonqualified stock option.

Resources

The following resources provide additional information on equity compensation, taxes and investing.

Equity Compensation

Fairmark Press Tax Guide for Investors (web site at www.fairmark.com). This is the first place to go for more information on this subject. You'll find a section where we'll post updates, corrections and clarifications to this book, and a message board where you can post comments and ask questions.

Stock Options: An Authoritative Guide to Incentive and Nonqualified Stock Options by Robert R. Pastore (PCM Capital Publishing, 2d ed. 1999). Ably covers much of the same material that this book addresses. It's considerably shorter than this book, so it covers fewer topics. Yet it also includes detailed numerical analysis of some planning alternatives, and includes an appendix that reproduces some pertinent regulations and rulings.

> The following books help with designing and running a stock option plan, and are not designed primarily to help the option holder.

The Entrepreneur's Guide to Equity Compensation (Foundation for Enterprise Development, 2d ed. 1998). This book gives an excellent overview of the different ways companies can provide an equity interest to their employees. It goes beyond stock and options to cover 401k plans, ESOPs and simulated equity plans. For more information visit their web site at www.fed.org.

The Stock Options Book (The National Center for Employee Ownership, 3d ed. 1999). This book is a series of essays, not a unified treatment of the subject. There's plenty of useful information here for people who are involved in equity compensation plan design and administration, but it isn't designed to be read by people who participate in such plans. For example, there are chapters on establishing and maintaining employee stock benefit programs, and accounting for stock-based compensation.

Stock Options: Beyond the Basics (The National Center for Employee Ownership, 1999). Like *The Stock Options Book* (see above), this is a book for option plan designers and administrators, not for option holders. As the title suggests, it covers advanced issues, such as federal securities law considerations and evergreen provisions. Their web site is located at www.nceo.org.

Taxes

Fairmark Press Tax Guide for Investors (web site at www.fairmark.com). We mentioned this above as a resource on the subject of equity compensation, but there's much more tax information for investors on this site, on topics from mutual funds to Roth IRAs.

The Motley Fool's Investment Tax Guide 2000: Smart Tax Strategies for Investors by Selena Maranjian and Roy A. Lewis (Motley Fool, Inc. 1999). Until we produce a print version of our web site, this is our choice for a tax guide aimed at investors. A lively, humorous approach takes the drudgery out of tax reading. For a review and ordering information:

www.fairmark.com/books/motley.htm

Tax Facts 2 on Investments (National Underwriter Company, new edition issued annually). Behind this unassuming title is a volume that provides detailed tax information on investments from stocks and bonds to equipment leasing and cattle. It's written for professionals, with many references to the Internal Revenue Code, revenue rulings and other authorities, yet it's a reasonably readable book in question and answer format. For a review and ordering information:

www.fairmark.com/books/taxfacts.htm

J.K. Lasser's Your Income Tax (annual series). If you're wondering which of the tax preparation manuals is the best, this is the one. Clear, thorough, accurate.

Personal Finance and Investing

Choices here are much more difficult because there are so many excellent books. Here are a few of the best.

The Only Investment Guide You'll Ever Need by Andrew Tobias (Harcourt Brace 1998). One of the all-time best sellers, and deservedly so. Readable and witty, yet commonsensical and authoritative. For a review and ordering information:

www.fairmark.com/books/tobias.htm

25 Myths You've Got to Avoid—If You Want to Manage Your Money Right by Jonathan Clements (Fireside 1998). The *Getting* Going columnist for the *Wall Street Journal* explains how the conventional wisdom can lead you down the wrong financial path. For a review and ordering information:

www.fairmark.com/books/clements.htm

The Motley Fool Investment Guide by David and Tom Gardner (Simon & Schuster 1996). Their approach is aggressive but highly successful—so far, at least. For a review and ordering information:

www.fairmark.com/books/gardner.htm

Greed is Good by Jonathan Hoenig (HarperBusiness 1999). A generation X take on how to accumulate wealth. Contains hundreds of cultural references, witty and often profane observations—and solid information and advice about saving and investing. For a review and ordering information:

www.fairmark.com/books/hoenig.htm

Index

Notes

Notes

Order Form

Order more copies of this book from our web site (**www.fairmark.com**), or by mailing or faxing a copy of this form.

Fax: (630) 434-0753   Mail: Fairmark Press Inc.
                                         P.O. Box 353
                                         Lisle, IL 60532

Your Purchase:

Number of copies of *Consider Your Options:* _____

Price: _____   ($23.95 per book)

Shipping   _____$3.00   (flat rate per order)

Total   _____

Illinois residents add $1.62 per book sales tax.

Ship to:

Name: _____

Address: _____

Address: _____

City, State, zip: _____

Phone: _____

Email: _____

Payment

____ Check   ____ VISA   ____ MasterCard

               ____ AMEX ____ Discover

Card number: _____

Exp. date: _____

Credit Card Info (if different from shipping)

Billing name: _____

Address: _____

Address: _____

City, State, zip: _____

Notes

Order Form

Order more copies of this book from our web site (**www.fairmark.com**), or by mailing or faxing a copy of this form.

Fax: (630) 434-0753

Mail: Fairmark Press Inc.
P.O. Box 353
Lisle, IL 60532

Your Purchase:

Number of copies of *Consider Your Options:* _____

Price: _____ ($23.95 per book)

Shipping _____$3.00 (flat rate per order)

Total _____

Illinois residents add $1.62 per book sales tax.

Ship to:

Name: _____

Address: _____

Address: _____

City, State, zip: _____

Phone: _____

Email: _____

Payment

____ Check   ____ VISA   ____ MasterCard
____ AMEX   ____ Discover

Card number: _____

Exp. date: _____

Credit Card Info (if different from shipping)

Billing name: _____

Address: _____

Address: _____

City, State, zip: _____